Dr. Angelika Schrand (PhD)
Anna Wilson

The Four Rooms of Change
The Changing Formula

Anna Wilson

Angelika Schrand (PhD)

THE FOUR ROOMS OF CHANGE

The Changing Formula

Imprint

Bibliographic information of the German National Library: The German National Library lists this publication in the German National Bibliography; detailed bibliographic data is available on the Internet at http://dnb.dnb.de.

Automated analysis of the work in order to obtain information, in particular about patterns, trends and correlations in accordance with §44b UrhG ("Text and Data Mining") is prohibited.

© 2025 Dr. Angelika Schrand, Anna Wilson (Eds)

Publisher: BoD · Books on Demand GmbH, Überseering 33, 22297 Hamburg, bod@bod.de

Print: Libri Plureos GmbH, Friedensallee 273, 22763 Hamburg

ISBN: 978-3-7693-2581-2

Content

Preface – Four Rooms the Changing Formula?

In today's world, it is more important than ever to learn how to deal with the many crises. The crises are here and are not getting any less, even if we all hope that they will disappear if possible. Uncertainty is increasing and we are very concerned about the alarming rise in listlessness and depression, especially among young people.

We realized that social interaction and shared experiences make us happier. We need this sense of community in our private lives as well as in society to achieve the necessary transformations, tackle social justice and the climate crisis and protect our democracy. This is emphasized by renowned scientists, but also by many initiatives such as InnerDevelopmentGoals.org and others. Only together we can overcome the enormous challenges facing us all and the individual – socially and in companies. Performance and innovation are brought about in a culture of inspiration, security and mutual appreciation and recognition, the basis for good cooperation.

But who hasn't experienced working with others in everyday life? Behaviour that annoys us, different ways of working and attitudes that we can't comprehend make everyday life difficult. But we can't change this, only our perspective on it. Or as Claes Janssen said: To agree to our disagreements.

If we can do this, we can utilize the strengths of diversity and use it as an opportunity, as a key success lever for companies and democratic societies. And this is made possible by working with the Four Rooms of Change Theory. It is not just a psychology for individuals, in fact it strengthens the sense of community and changes the culture of collaboration. It provides what is needed to achieve greater contentment and inspiration as an individual, as a team and as an organization – the prerequisite for productivity and innovation.

So far there is nothing in the original by Claes Janssen on the internet. Many plagiarized works refer to him without using the core of the theory and his work. We want to honour the great work of Claes Janssen and support his wish that as many people as possible have the chance to use this practical psychology in their everyday life and that we all achieve more life contentment and reduce conflicts within ourselves, in our professional and social environment.

Purpose of the book

This book is intended to provide insights into the development of the Four Rooms of Change Theory, which are currently only available in the Swedish original, and to provide background information on Claes Janssen, the developer of the theory who, in our view, deserves to be recognized internationally for his life's work.

In Chapter 1 we describe the development process of the entire Four Rooms of Change Theory. In terms of content, the individual steps are described to the extent that they become clear as links and process steps. However, not all steps were developed one-to-one as a straightforward process, instead there was some back- and forward movement. In this book, the steps are presented one after the other to be able to understand the interconnectedness of the elements of the theory.

In Chapter 2 we deepen the understanding of the Four Rooms of Change Theory.

In Chapter 3 we show the different use cases.

In Chapter 4 we link and compare the theory to other theories.

We would like to thank everyone who has contributed to this book.

As Coauthors: Birgit Freitag, Wiebke Steinel, Giuliano Tarditi, Jens Witte, Dr. Doris Yuan. All Coauthors are therefore identified by name. You will find all the authors and a brief description of them in the appendix at the end of the book.

Andreas Schöneberg, who developed the Cover. Dr. Jari Grosse-Ruyken who inspired us with the title -The Changing Formula, all colleagues from CONTUR and Janssen´s Model® who contributed with feedback, ideas and just with inspiration so that we can finalize this book.

Four Rooms of Change

the Changing Formula

you´ll see it works

If you want to learn about how you can work with the instruments, you´ll find the QR Codes and links on Page 140.

Strängnäs 2021

Claes Janssen PhD, (1937-2024), was a Swedish psychologist, re-
searcher, and author, renowned for his innovative work in the
field of change management. Ulla Janssen (1945-2022) started in
2000 to bring the Four Rooms to schools.

The Story of
Claes Janssens
Development
of the Theory

1. The Story of Claes Janssens Development of the Theory

Dr. Angelika Schrand

The Four Rooms Theory means so much more than just the model.

If you enter Four Rooms in search engines, you will find various interpretations of the Four Rooms. Or if you ask experienced change consultants, coaches and managers, you recognize that many are familiar with the Four Rooms, often also they name the plagiarized version: The Change House, The Four Rooms Apartments or The House of Change. Claes Janssen is often named as the originator who developed it and he himself says to the various interpretations:

"Unfortunately, it can happen, that what you are shown is a piece of plagiarism – a four-square diagram with the same psychological content as the Four Rooms has, perhaps with changed names in one or two of the frames, perhaps even that. ... The point of plagiarism is hard to see. "[1]

In this section we outline the development of the Four Rooms theory by Claes Janssen, and it becomes evident that the entire theory provides much more than just the international well-known model and that the many interpretations of the Four Rooms do not represent full potential. Or, that it is used in some way that it can even be harmful to the organization.

"Psychology is a damned stupid science."[2]

To be able to contextualize the further development of the theory and the instruments, the quote mentioned in the title is enlightening. It is from the father of Claes Janssen who hated psychology and Claes Janssen remarked:

"My father was a realist with a strong preference for simplicity. I preferred complexity and depth. Whereas I was concerned with the truth, my father saw the consequences. Will this convince? If this is taken to be the truth, what will be the consequence? Seeing things with my father's eyes convinced me that it was not good enough for a psychological theory to be scientific, original, creative. It had to make one feel good, if one took it to be the truth, and lived by it. It had to be integrative." [3]

This explains with which intention the further development of the theory, the instruments and further development has been developed - not only to have a scientific theory, but it should also be of practical use and benefit.

Why the movie 491 was the starting point

It began in 1964 with the movie 491, which Vilgat Sjöman produces after a novel by Lars Görling. The film is about the attempt to make six abandoned young people from Stockholm socially acceptable again. In 491 the liberal approach to education did not work out. It escalated and the police intervened. The film was censored and a big debate started. Some found the film harmfully exciting and others brutalizing. This led to research to which Claes Janssen, as a young psychology student, contributed. They investigated in the *will of censor* to understand why people reject something and others do less. At the age of 24 he could make his first original study sponsored by the Swedish Film Institute. This was the starting point of the development of the Four Rooms of Change Theory.

13

The Development of Personal Dialectics as the core of the Theory

Claes Janssen read Colin Wilson's book – *The Outsider*, while working for the Swedish Film Institute from 1964-1966 to investigate the attitudes that led to the rejection of films. Colin Wilson's book is about the experience and feelings of being an outsider who stands for truth.

"It was a most fortunate coincidence - a turning point in my life, in fact. Outsiders turned out to be against censorship. Outsiders and Self-Censors had different conceptions of reality and different conceptions of themselves." [4]

Claes Janssen's aim was to make the perception of being an outsider measurable and this resulted in the discovering of two existential stances – a dilemma which he describes as:

"...whether to "censor" one's experience, so as to feel or been seen as normal, so as to belong, or to fight this self-censorship, but then suffer from the confusion and sense of being different, or "odd", which the non-conformist stance of the Outsider frequently creates, at first." [5]

His own experiences and the exchange with others showed that you do not consistently have this feeling of unreality, of standing next to others and not belonging. Instead, you feel very comfortable in other situations, you feel like you belong. There are also situations in which you are completely in the flow, such as when you go horse riding or sailing for example. But how can this be measured in a scientifically reliable way?

It took him more than 10 years, until 1975, from the first discovery of the two existential stances in 1964 to the realization of the Outsider Scale because the idea that there are not just the poles, but that there is also an integration, as you feel different as described above, made the task more difficult. Integration is meant in the sense of cooperation between the two sides as parts of a whole, a person, a social system like a family, team or organization. He quotes Goethe *"Twin souls live in the breast. "*

He often mentioned that C.G. Jung is the major shoulder he stands on. The work of a lot of other psychologists, authors, psychotherapists like Colin Wilson, R.D. Laing, Abraham Maslow, Ernest Rossi, Stanislav Grof and later also Carl Rogers, Eric Berne, Peter Koestenbaum and Douglas McGregor as examples helped to deepen different perspectives on his theory.

The research started with the interpretation of the Outsider's experience, which has been described as a symptom or hidden will:

> 1.Sensitivity
> 2. Preference for feeling and/or intuition in a society dominated by thought and sensation
> 3. Creativity
> 4. As a conflict between a humanistic conscience and an authoritarian superego
> 5. A will to be free, or at least free from one's sex role.[6]

Through a series of research steps, he succeeded in developing the Outsider questionnaire and its evaluation process. This was the subject of his doctoral thesis. (A detailed description can be found in the thesis Personal Dialectics published in 1975).

From a complex theory to the simple one made by consensus

In his analysis of the results of the questionnaire Claes Janssen identified two poles. He named the poles as NO answerers and YES answerers. He correlated his questionnaire with measures of creativity, authoritarianism, conventional/unconventional conception of reality, preference for status quo or change and a lot more and that made it possible for him to develop a scale which he called later "Outsider Scale". Claes Janssen was able to take some items from the research of Frank Y. Barron, a pioneer in the study of creativity, conformity and non-conformity. He also referred to Viktor E. Frankl, whose theory was based on the assumption that the primary motivational force is the search for meaning. Together with the researchers mentioned in the previous chapter, these basic principles enabled him to better understand the two poles, which we would like to illustrate in the following example.

If you are asked what your life is about, what the strongest motive for you has been (whether you have thought it out or not), could you answer something like this: a search for truth, or search for personal freedom and a heightened sense of existence?

You can answer the question with YES or NO and the more you answer YES to the 24 questions of the questionnaire, the more you tend to be a YES answerer and with more NO you tend to be a NO answerer. And this leads to a different attitude to life or existential stances. This is what we describe in chapter (2.1) in more detail, and this influences how we deal with change.

The aim of making the outsider's experience measurable was therefore within reach, but not satisfactory for Claes Janssen.

"My theory was not good enough. I felt. It did not make me feel good. It seemed that however I described the two existential stances and the conflict between them, it was in words that made one of them seem preferable, right and the other wrong. If I entered intuitively into one of the stances, describing it sympathetically, with respect for that choice, it was if I thereby questioned the alternative one-and vice versa. It was a Scyalla or Charybids dilemma." [7]

The breakthrough came with an experiment. After a decisive hint from R.D. Laing that he was probably not the only one who felt this dilemma, but that other people would too, he started the experiment.

He collected many descriptions of two hypothetical people who were each at the end of the two poles and was surprised at how many agreeing or disagreeing descriptions emerged. This made the conflict transparent between the hypothetical people and this led to another question: Are these two characters real? Claes Janssen answers the following:

"The common answer to the question: Are those characters real? Will be both yes and no.

The agreement reached is that it frequently seems as if they were real. The truth is relative. We are all a mixture of both, but some might seem to be nine tenth No and one tenth Yes, some nine tenth yes and one tenth No.

Situational factors are emphasized as a rule. We act as No Answeres or Yes Answeres in particular situations - so even the nine tenth Yes person will act now and then, as a No Answerer." [8]

This led to the realization that both tendencies are in us and depend on the situation. And here the preference is added to which direction we tend to be influenced in our thoughts and actions. We go deeper into this in chapter 2.1.

Another important aspect is that these two poles lead to tensions within us and must be negotiated. Here is an example to illustrate this: How do I behave if I think someone is being treated unfairly? Do I intervene because it is not right, or do I keep quiet because I do not want to attract attention and do not want to get involved in the conflict?

This is what he outlined in the book Personal Dialectics, published in 1975.

The Meaning of Personal Dialectics

Dialectics has a double meaning: On the one hand it means tension between opposites *"...the tension between the perspectives*

*of the Yes Answerer and the No Answerer, which represent two
diametrically opposed ways of being, of perceiving oneself, others
and society" and on the other hand the art of dialogue "refers to
the possibility of a dialogue between both perspectives."* [9]

We will deepen the understanding of dialectics in Chapter 2.1.

For further understanding, we would like to add at this point that
these tensions between diametrically different perspectives on
life do not only arise within individuals, but also between people
in all forms in which they come together, from families to work
teams and, moreover, in society, which surely each of us can ob-
serve in attitudes to current social issues, for example migration
policy or sustainability and how to deal with.

To Agree on our Disagreements

The emergence of tensions and resulting conflicts could be explained, but the next step was to understand how we can better
deal with these inner tensions, with our disagreements and how
we act, if we disagree, how others think and behave. The conflicts
were visible but the question that arose was how to deal with it
when someone has a completely different attitude, if he/she
does not see it as their strongest motive to search for the truth
on the one side of the Outsider Scale (the Yes answerer) or on the
other side of the scale (as a No answerer) where the sense of security and belonging to a group is much more important to them.
This leads to different assessments of what every one of us experiences every day, for example how people see activists who are
fighting for a particular goal.

Based on the understanding of dialectics which Claes Janssen
took from C.G. Jung:

*"who considers that creative change happened through the con-
flict, when they were equal, seen as equal."* [10]

This assumption is fundamental for understanding and working with the Four Rooms of Change Theory. Both perspectives on life are to be understood as equally valuable and neither is better than the other. *The magnificent both/and expression* of C.G. Jung is a basing idea for the development of the theory and the perception enables interpretation of the two opposing poles in everyone, between people and in the society.

So far, he had asked individuals about two hypothetical people. The next step was to analyze how it will be experienced when a group is doing it together.

He worked with groups using two hypothetical people and let them describe positive and negative behaviors and attitudes. Typically, the following descriptions are given, and it becomes obvious that many conflicts arise from the different views on life. The matrix shows the respective poles, i.e. how they perceive themselves as positive (NO+) and (YES+) and what they perceive as negative at the other end of the scale.

The Matrix of Disagreements [11]

NO+ (No about No)	YES+ (Yes about Yes)
<ul><li>realistic</li><li>calm, strong, confident</li><li>stable, reliable</li><li>practical, sensible, matter of fact</li><li>friendly, cooperative</li><li>takes it easy</li></ul>	<ul><li>independent</li><li>sensitive, imaginative, artistic</li><li>a seeker, open to change</li><li>courageous, wants challenge</li><li>non-conforming, radical</li><li>open, honest, spontaneous</li><li>creative</li></ul>
NO- (Yes about No)	**YES- (No about Yes)**
<ul><li>controlled</li><li>conventional</li><li>shallow, hypocritical</li><li>boring, stiff</li><li>afraid of change</li><li>could not get in touch with feelings</li><li>authoritarian</li><li>mechanical, robotic,</li><li>unreal, cynical</li></ul>	<ul><li>eccentric</li><li>unrealistic, a dreamer, out of touch with reality</li><li>a loner</li><li>selfish, self-centered</li><li>a troublemaker, pain in the ass,</li><li>moody, uncertain</li><li>lacks self-confidence,</li><li>lost, drifting</li><li>bleeding hearts</li></ul>

With this experiment, he proved that groups could work out the theory together and another significant effect became visible. When the group worked it out together, the ability to consciously deal with one's disagreements is strengthened, and a collective feeling and immediate enthusiasm is created through joint development. It took him about seven years to really finalize the process of how to do the *Introduction to the Four Rooms.* And even today in 2025, the theory is being jointly developed in the same way.

A presentation and explanation of the theory does not have the effects as building it together, the process of developing the theory convinces in itself, it integrates, creates a common knowledge and collective feeling. And this is what we, all the authors in this book, experience every time we run the Introduction Process. That is why we are convinced that it is really helpful in today's world. For individuals, for all kinds of social systems and society.

The development of the Four Rooms: Frames of Mind

By changing the perspective from describing people to describing them from the inside out, emotions or feelings become visible. People describe them in the following matrix.

Matrix Frames of Mind and the name of the respective state of mind [12]

NO+	YES+
<ul><li>confident</li><li>calm</li><li>effective</li><li>feeling good about myself</li><li>useful</li><li>comfortable</li><li>belonging</li></ul>	<ul><li>eager</li><li>strong</li><li>open</li><li>alive</li><li>independent</li><li>courageous</li><li>growing</li><li>warm</li><li>creative</li></ul>
NO-	YES-
<ul><li>irritated</li><li>tense</li><li>bored</li><li>determined</li><li>hard</li><li>hidden</li><li>frozen</li><li>indifferent</li><li>critical</li><li>hostile</li><li>a prisoner of necessity</li></ul>	<ul><li>troubled</li><li>alone</li><li>frustrated</li><li>split, confused</li><li>no self-confidence</li><li>helpless</li><li>doubtful</li><li>burnt out</li><li>afraid</li><li>sad</li><li>left out</li><li>paralyzed</li><li>rootless</li></ul>

In this intermediate step on the way to developing the Four Rooms of Change, it also shows that the character of the rooms remains the same. *"The mood, or the psychological energy and tension pattern within each frame is the same, although now seen from within."* [13]

On the way to the Four Rooms of Change model, the names for the frames of mind were very clear for Claes Janssen:

> NO- he calls **Self-Censorship or Denial**,
> YES- he names **Confusion** and
> YES+ was named as **Inspiration or Renewal.**

Something was missing he thought, because nobody wants to live in the three states described above.

"It seemed that my theory lacked one gear, namely "Relax, take it easy"- There was no compromise in the theory. There was no place for making mistakes and still like oneself, either." [14]

He found the right name on an advertising poster for Lipton tea in the London Underground Railway.

Contentment, as a state for satisfaction (with something). The missing piece of the Puzzle was there, and he developed the Four Rooms of Change model, with the experiences and feelings of people as shown in the matrix. He decided to use the name of the Four Rooms as a description for the different states of mind to make it easily understandable. In chapter 2.4 we describe the Four Rooms model in detail.

The Change Cycle through the Four Rooms

As things are changing, things are going wrong, we are moving out of the psychological state of Contentment. We all move through the four psychological states of mind, which are named as the Four Rooms of Change, which are in each of us.

The next challenge was to integrate the time perspective and how we go through the rooms and in what order.

There were several theories and scientific research that Claes Janssen could refer to when we are thrown out of Contentment by a dramatic sudden case, like death in our close family. He mentions as an example Johann Cullberg (1977) and Daniel Levinson and their discovering, that all men go through a so-called mid-life crisis. He also uses Ernest Rossi and his publication Break Out Heuristic as a decisive help in explaining the movements through the Four Rooms.[16]

But not all changes are necessary due to a dramatic sudden cause. Changes can also happen gradually and here, too, it is necessary to move through all the rooms to return to Contentment, and the order how to move through the rooms is the same.

Another insight was that, depending on the context, you can be in different rooms - in the family, for example, in the room of Contentment, while at work you can be in Confusion. (See Chapter 2.5.).

The Matrix of Change[17]

NO+ CONTENTMENT	YES+ INSPIRATION or RENEWAL
Adjustment. My present situation feels good enough as it is. Relaxed, effortless self-control. Attention focused on the here & now, no marked self-reflection. "I am ok, you are ok." Feeling "average" in the sense of not being special. Being there.	Creative change. Integration. A sense of "getting it all together". Insights, aha-experiences. Feeling freely and expressed. Intense experience of the here & now, with self-reflection: I participate and observe that I am participating. Strong feelings of community. Energy. Radical ideas, a desire to make things happen.
NO- SELF-CENSORSHIP or DENIAL Pseudo-adjustment. Self-discipline with focus on completing a certain task or defending a certain pattern or status quo. No clear feelings. I am in control but uptight. The here & now (if experienced at all) feels empty and mechanical. Irritation. Attention concentrated on the task felt to be necessary, on the rules and/or my image in other's eyes, on not losing face. On tactical considerations, etc.	**YES- CONFUSION** Maladjustment. Something is or feels wrong here & now, but I do what to do to make things right. Tense, negative self-consciousness with feelings of inferiority and doubts, self-centered. Chaos. Dialectical YES/NO conflicts within or without. Feelings in a clinch. A sense of unreality.

Based on his motivation described earlier in the book, developing a theory that only describes is not good enough. The theory has to help people in everyday lives. The Matrix of Change was further developed to provide concrete guidance to increase wellbeing time for everyone. The well-being time can be defined with the following formula:

We describe these steps and guide on how to increase wellbeing time in chapter 2.6.

The Problem-Situation Matrix or the Matrix of the Will[16]

Building on the developed matrixes, Claes Janssen worked out another matrix: the Problem-Situation Matrix which he also called the Matrix of the Will.

Claes Janssen explained the further development as follows:

"The difference between the first and the second matrix was the time perspective. The YES/NO matrix described attitudes or existential stances, seen as relatively permanent. The second, converted matrix described the states, or frames of mind, seen as stages in a change cycle. If we take one more step and see all four frames of mind as present at the same times, they can be perceived as functions or aspects of a problem situation."

The Problem-Situation Matrix[18]

(NO+) SITUATION	(YES+) POSSIBILITIES
▪ What is the problem situation? ▪ Who am I, who has Problems ▪ What is good enough as it is in Problem-situation-what am I content with?	▪ Factors of strength: What am I good at? ▪ Success memories. ▪ Alternatives of action, ideas. ▪ Brainstorm! Alternative reactions? ▪ Who can help me? ▪ Courage that furthers is the courage to...
(NO-) DIFFICULTIES	**(YES-) WILL**
▪ Weaknesses: What am I bad at? ▪ Obstacles, reality conditions, "alienation factors": What knowledge or know how do I lack? ▪ Conflicts external: YES/NO? Conflicts? ▪ What is just right, self-censorship in the Problem Situation ▪ Risks: The worst that can happen is... ▪ What (self-) discipline is necessary?	▪ What do I do, who am I in this Problem-Situation, what do I want? ▪ Suggested motto: "I have a dream..." ▪ What are my feelings in this Problem Situation? ▪ Peripheral associations? ▪ Moving to a time in the future when the Problem is solved: How will I feel? What will I lose? ▪ Conflicts internal YES/NO? ▪ Temptations. ▪ What do I not want? What am I afraid of? What do I have to give up?

The matrix is not called the **problem-solution matrix**: it is called the **problem-situation matrix**, and this has a special meaning.

If we focus too much on the problem when describing the problem situation, it regularly happens that we end up in the room of self-censorship or denial. Working with the matrix does not take place step by step, but thoughts jump from one field to another. An answer to a question will trigger an answer to another, so reflection and an inner dialogue happens and leads to ideas to solve the problem, while considering the context. The **WILL *is discovered*** in the situational context of difficulties and possibilities and the **WILL *to change*** things is activated.

Four Rooms in Organizations

As already explained on the previous pages, the YES/NO conflict does not only occur within a person, but it also occurs between individuals and at a societal level.

The collaborative development of the theory develops a common knowledge. And what Claes Janssen observed in his years of practical experience is that it creates a spirit and energy in the teams.

He thought it could be useful:

"-to describe an organization's present situation,

-to de-dramatize the YES/NO conflicts,

-to catalyze change, create action". [19]

Companies need both effectiveness and renewal in order to survive in the long term. And this is where the connection to the rooms of Contentment and Inspiration becomes very clear.

It is important for individuals in Contentment to have clear goals and to achieve them. When this happens, confidence and trust within the company increases, just as self-confidence increases on an individual level.

A person in censorship denies that there is a problem, which is exactly what happens in companies. Problems are censored and not discussed openly, but often on the floor.

A person in Confusion wants to change but does not yet know how or what exactly he/she wants to do. Transferring to the company level, this means that the strategy, goals and responsibilities are not clear, and this leads to uncertainty.

A person in the room of Inspiration is full of energy and initiative because these feelings are subjectively experienced as meaningful living.

If the company has a common purpose, is open to new ideas and has flexibility and room for individual development, employee commitment increases. Claes Janssen developed the Organizational Analysis Barometer until 1985. The now called "Situational Analysis" uses 40 questions to measure "internal quality" or corporate culture.

Alos here the handling of the instrument is crucial for success. From the conviction that:

"My conviction is that quality, personal life quality as well as organizational quality is combined"[20]

Claes Janssen also uses it in collaboration with organizational development consultants and particularly noteworthy here is the cooperation with Marvin Weisboard starting in 1978. In the book of Marvin Weisbord "Productive Workplaces" which was published in 1985 the Four Rooms of Change Theory has been described in various contexts. For Claes Janssen it was elementary the way in which the survey was organized and the process of involving the respondents in the processing of the survey results. The direct evaluation and derivation of improvement initiatives always takes place together with the respondents. More information on this can be found in chapter 2.7.

Further Developments

Claes Janssen's work does not end with this theory; he developed various other approaches, and written reflections are available, but not published for in-depth study.

However, this story ends here, as we hope that the processual presentation of the theory will make it possible to comprehend how the individual building blocks of the theory were developed and interact with each other. As mentioned, we invite you to dive deeper into the theory in the next chapters and "read" the practical implementation and benefits, which of course cannot substitute experience.

The Theory:
Practical Everyday
Psychology

2. The Theory: Practical Everyday Psychology

Dr. Angelika Schrand, Anna Wilson

2.1 The two approaches to life and their impact on our lives

Claes Janssen developed the Personal Dialectics Self-Test, which helps you discover your own preferences and where you are on the Dialectic Scale. In his theory development, Claes Janssen identifies the two poles that he calls Yes answerers and No answerers, which represent two approaches to life. The question we want to answer in this chapter: What does this mean? And how does it affect our life, our development and how we act in changing situations with ourselves and how we interact with others.

We will answer these central questions by following two purposes: One purpose is to show how the knowledge of the Four Rooms of Change Theory helps every one of us to increase our "Wellbeing Time". It is demonstrated in this simple formula by Claes Janssen:

The second purpose is to improve the art of conversation between the two approaches to life. The Yes Answerer and the No Answerer, which represent two diametrically opposed ways of being, of perceiving oneself, others and society, in ourselves, in teams and in society.

Before we dive deeper into those two purposes, first of all we will further explain the term Personal Dialectics as a central component of Claes Janssens theory.

Personal Dialectics

The title Personal Dialectics refers to the tension between the NO and YES perspectives, which are two completely opposite ways of perceiving oneself, others and society.

The word dialectics means on the one hand:

The tension between opposites: the thesis, the antithesis and their possible synthesis.

As an inner conflict it can be experienced as a struggle between good judgement and force of initiative. It can appear as a conflict between the status quo and change and can be described as the conflict between independence, creativity, risk-taking and conformity, between the desire to be oneself and the wish to belong.

Claes Janssen simply called it he **Yes/No conflict**:

"We experience it daily as an inner conflict, in miniature, as the question: Shall I say what I think here and now, show how I feel, do what I want to do- or would it be wiser to censor myself"[1]

This conflict occurs

— between individuals, who in one another's eyes embody the respective ways of being.

- in teams. It becomes visible because on the one hand, you have people who insist on following the rules, processes, and standards. On the other hand, you have people who want to innovate because they think it is more effective.
- in society, where it manifests as different opinions about how to be set up. One example is the discussion about how to deal with climate crisis: To become an activist and fight for more radical change and to focus on not changing too fast.

On the other hand, dialectics means the expression, the art of dialogue. It refers to the possibility of an art of dialogue between both perspectives.

The art of dialogue refers to the skillful and thoughtful exchange of ideas, thoughts, and feelings between two or more people. It is more than just talking, valuing different perspectives and being open to new ideas. It is about active listening, understanding, and responding in a way that fosters meaningful and productive communication.

The DIALECTIC SCALE – Tension between opposites

Tensions often arise between these two different perspectives on life, particularly if the people are pronounced Yes or No answerers.

We can illustrate the different perspectives on life on a bell curve (the dialectic scale).

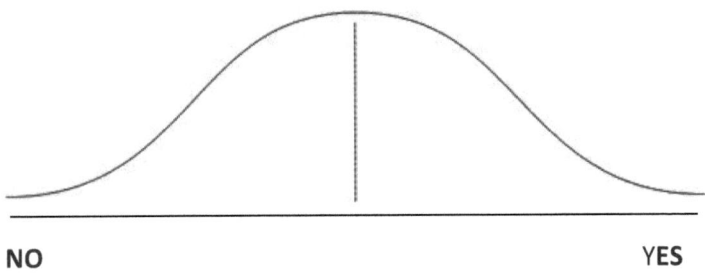

NO   **YES**

Those on the left side of the scale respond NO often
Those on the right side respond YES often

With Personal Dialectics (the self-test consists of 24 questions) you can position yourself on the scale depending on how many questions you answered with yes. The position on the scale is not fixed and a normal distribution depending on the situation is given. And what is important:

Neither position on the scale is **better or worse** than the other. As we see on the bell curve, most people have both. It is important to be able to access both sides.

We need both: YES and NO pieces.
YES to find yourself and NO to function practically.

The intention is to have a high integration to reach your personal optimal point. The word integration means roughly the interplay between the separate parts of a whole. One example to illustrate when the No and Yes pieces are not aligned:

If you are in group of people, e.g. your friends, and you have the feeling, you have to wear a mask, you cannot be yourself and you do not show how you feel, you can sense an inner conflict. Your No pieces dominate in this situation, and you do not feel relaxed and content. You feel rather uncomfortable and blocked.

This indicates that you are according to the Matrix of Change of change in the Room of denial and according to the simple "well-being" formula, this increases the minus time.

Working with the Personal Dialectics helps to identify where you are on the dialectic scale and through deepening integration questions you can discover the fields in which you are able to (if you like) *free yourself*. This is an expression Claes Janssen often uses as a chance when using the theory.

To work with the theory also changes the perception and increases the ability to *Agree on your Disagreements*.

2.2 The Matrix of Disagreements

As described in the former chapter, the further step of the development of the theory is the Matrix of Disagreement. The position on the Outsider Scale has not only an impact on us but also on how we deal with others. The following matrix is composed of key words which are typically used when Yes answerers and No answerers describe themselves and each other.

Matrix of Disagreements

NO + (no about no)	YES + (yes about yes)
- realistic - calm, strong, confident - stable, reliable - practical, sensible, matter of fact - friendly, cooperative - takes it easy	- independent - sensitive, imaginative, - artistic - a seeker, open to change - courageous, wants challenge - non-conforming, radical - open honest, spontaneous - creative
NO- (yes about no)	YES- (no about yes)
- controlled - conventional, - shallow, hypocritical - boring, stiff - afraid of change - could not in touch with feelings - authoritarian - mechanical, robotic, unreal - cynical	- eccentric - unrealistic, a dreamer, out of touch with reality - a loner - selfish, self-centered - a troublemaker, pain in the ass - moody, uncertain, lacks self confidence - lost, drifting - bleeding hearts

The matrix somewhat exaggerates the contrasts and underlines the tendency to see one another in a negative light.

This tendency to see each other's negative traits can be interpreted as a natural form of *self-defense*. It may also be rooted in what is referred to in psychological terms as *projection*. Projection is when we attribute the emotions and qualities that we ourselves possess to others but that we are unaware of or even afraid to acknowledge.

It is likely that we construct the image of *the other* on emotions that we have personally experienced. In other words, NO respondents, when they have leaned towards YES, have felt alone, confused and so on- and the YES respondents, when they have leaned towards NO, have experienced rigidness, insensitivity and superficialness.

These perceptions of others and the associated reluctance to admit one's own attributes do not infrequently lead to conflicts in social relationships, from families to professional teams.

Examples in the corporate context demonstrate this clearly: People who are on the Yes answerer side of the Personal Dialectic Scale are often creative and want to implement their ideas, even at the risk of changing *rules and habits* they don´t adapt. Very much to the displeasure of others, for whom this is more important.

People who do not jump on the changes are considered resistance fighters. For them stability, certainty and belonging are important.

The recognition and acceptance that there are two different ways of looking at life, and that neither one nor the other is better, leads to a different kind of dialogue. This is what can be achieved by using the Four Rooms of Change Theory that will be explained in the following chapters. And on top of that utilizing diversity is a strength, as we also know from Diversity & Inclusion approaches.

2.3 The Four Frames of Mind

We are shifting the perspective. Instead of looking at the words in the matrix of disagreement descriptions of people seen from the outside, let's look at them as descriptions of states of being or moods. We can then ask ourselves how this feels from within. These are words often used when describing what being in different quadrants looks like.[2]

NO +	YES +
confident, calm, effective, feeling good about myself, relaxed, willing to compromise, uncomplicated, resting, splendid "a good girl" collected, useful, industrious, belonging, comfortable, optimistic, satisfied, sleepy	eager, strong, open, alive, able to do what I want, light, "like a balloon", intelligent, independent, growing, warm, glowing, vibrant, creative, "high", "insightful" "groovy" in touch with God, in touch with the Devil, ecstatic, "faith, hope and love" courageous, rich, infinite
NO-	YES-
Irritated, tense, bored, calculating, withdrawn, married(!) tough, determined, stating the facts, square, superior, deliberating, poor, mean, like an impostor, abstract, hard, hidden, frozen, hesitant, entangled, gnawing, fettered, "a prisoner on necessity," harsh, indifferent, cynical, uniformed, critical, hostile, pornographic, condemned	troubled, alone, frustrated, split, anxious, misty, different, confused, no self-confidence, restless, worthless, helpless, a failure, raging, ambivalent, rootless, inferior, uncertain, doubtful, afraid, sad, left out, "no one understands me", burnt out, paralyzed, "why do I live?" torn, lost, fragmented, in chaos

The mood or the psychological energy and tension pattern in this matrix is the same as the "Matrix of Disagreements" but seen from within. Depending on the situation, we find ourselves in a different frame. If we now expand the context in the sense on how we behave in the respective frame regarding change, we come to the matrix that is widely known. The Four Rooms of Change Matrix or as Claes Janssen also mentioned it, the four states as rooms in the existential "soul house" we all live in.

2.4 The Four Rooms of Change

The Four Rooms[3]

NO + CONTENTMENT	YES + INSPIRATION or RENEWAL
<ul><li>Adjustment.</li><li>My present situation feels good enough as it is.</li><li>Relaxed, effortless self-control.</li><li>Attention focused on the here & now,</li><li>no marked self-reflection. "I'm ok, you are ok"</li><li>Feeling "average" in the sense of not being special.</li><li>Being there.</li></ul>	<ul><li>Creative change. Integration.</li><li>A sense of "getting it all together".</li><li>Insights, aha-experiences</li><li>Feeling freely felt and expressed.</li><li>Intense experience of the here & now, with self-reflection: I participate and observe that I am participating</li><li>Strong feelings of community.</li><li>Energy. Radical ideas, a desire to make things happen.</li></ul>
NO- SELF-CENSORSHIP or DENIAL	**YES- CONFUSION**
<ul><li>Pseudo-adjustment.</li><li>Self-discipline with focus on completing a certain task or defending a certain pattern or status quo.</li></ul>	<ul><li>Maladjustment.</li><li>Something is or feels wrong here & now, but I do what to do to make things right.</li><li>Tense, negative self-consciousness with feelings</li></ul>

■ No clear feelings. I am in control but uptight. ■ The here and now (if experienced at all) feels empty and mechanical. ■ Irritation. ■ Attention concentrated on the task felt to be necessary, on the rules and /or my image in other's eyes, on not losing face. ■ On tactical considerations.	of inferiority and doubts, self-centered. ■ Chaos. ■ Dialectical Yes/No Conflicts within or without. Feelings in a clinch. ■ A sense of unreality

A Four Roomer within us all

The words that describe a pronounced NO and YES respondent can actually apply to all of us. A person can, for instance, feel self-confident and realistic. But at the same time, be sensitive and of the opinion that it is wise to protest against society instead of simply adapting. A person can be afraid of what people will think and censor themselves, but also feel alone, unhappy and self-absorbed.

> **The above image basically describes every human being and illustrates various ups and downs of life.**
>
> **We all have access to these four "rooms".**
>
> **But we spend different amounts of time in these rooms.**

Another way of describing the difference is to say that each person's centre is in different rooms, and we experience our stays differently. We can call the different rooms for CONTENTMENT (or adjustment), CENSORSHIP (or pseudo-adjustment), CONFUSION (or maladjustment) and INSPIRATION (or creative change).

These rooms describe different states. The words in the four boxes offer a kind of holistic description of a person who is in the "room", or in the state. It is likely that a person who is in CONTENTMENT, is perceived as realistic, a person in CENSORSHIP is perceived as insensitive, a person in CONFUSION is perceived as self-absorbed and a person in INSPIRATION as open and creative.

2.5 Movements

As explained before, everyone has access to each of the four rooms. As people develop, they move between the rooms. People move between the rooms as they develop. This movement could look like this:

Imagine a person, a man in this case, who is content. His life has pretty much what he wants it to have. It's OK. He can relax in his life. He lacks nothing. He takes things as they come. He likes his partner, their friends, his work, his city and his boat, if he has one. He doesn't look with envy on other boats when he's out sailing in his own; that the boat is not perfect does not stop him from loving it. This is CONTENTMENT.

But now something has happened. It could be anything. Maybe a change at work so that he no longer fully enjoys what he does. Or that his relationship has lost its spark, that they can no longer talk about important things or laugh together, and instead, a slow silence starts to spread.

The man has now lost his CONTENTMENT. Something is lacking in his life, but he doesn't quite know what. He continues to consider himself to be a person who is content. He pretends that he is satisfied. He doesn't take things as they come anymore, but he pretends to. He censors himself. This makes him tense, unpleasant, puts him in a bad mood, all of which makes him insensitive since he is afraid to delve into his emotions. When he censors himself, he also censors others. If he wants to forget something, he must first, for example, quiet his wife when she wants to talk about things. He is now in the authoritarian room, in CENSORSHIP (denial).

When someone is there, they typically don't know they're there. The reason is that we are afraid of the emotions and conflicts which would move us to the next room, CONFUSION, when we breach our censorship. CONFUSION is home to loneliness, insecurity, difficulty making contact and self-absorption. It's a scary place to be. No one wants to go there. If our man pulls back, if he thinks that he's taking himself too seriously and tries not to, he gets stuck in the authoritarian attitude. He becomes rigid. If he doesn't, if he thinks what the heck, life is tough, and conflicts are a part of life. Feeling weak, sad, alone, afraid, confused, or angry will probably release something. If he thinks that it's natural to go through a crisis and literally dump all the pieces of his life in one big mess on the floor in his room and settles down to look at them. Then he can discover what is lacking – what dreams and desires he has censored out of his life, what weaknesses he is trying to avoid, and what potential in his present life that he is not realizing.

He recognizes that it may be wiser to try to get through the difficulties.

This self-analysis gives him new insights, probably even allows him to experience inspiration, connection and an elevated sense of purpose. Now he can move to the next room, INSPIRATION. Here he is honest, inquisitive, sensitive, open to changes and creative. In this room he has a strong connection with the here and now. In his state of inspiration, others might find him difficult to deal with, particularly if they are still censoring and defending the status quo.

This openness, honesty and creativity contains a wealth of possibilities, energy and drive. But the possibilities are difficult to bring back into everyday reality. It is possible to change things, but not completely, and it takes time. New compromises prove necessary, and it means having to give up some possibilities to realize others. So, a degree of openness, honesty and inspiration is lost again.

Hopefully, our man is wise enough to accept this and understand that a realizable insight is better than ten wise, deep truths that will never reach completion. And now, the man is back in a new CONTENTMENT. He has replaced some of the poor compromises for others, he has a new status quo, a new balance, most probably one that is freer than the old one, more in harmony with himself.

Crisis and Change

Crises are brought about by drastic changes in life circumstances, like divorces and illnesses, such as the loss of sight. Blind people describe how it's essential to "bury your seeing self" before you can start to build a new life. Divorces and illnesses typically bring about crisis. Other crises are simply natural transitions from one phase to another in the cycle of life. It seems that there are elements of a crisis in a one-year-old's transition from crawling to walking. The expanded freedom of movement and independence is associated with certain risk-taking: you can fall and hurt yourself. The transition later in life, from cowering for authorities to standing up for your own convictions, embodies the same conflict. We also have the midlife crisis at the halfway point in life – which seems to have a miniature equivalent in the "holiday crisis" that occurs at the halfway point of a holiday and the realization it will soon come to an end, and this is as good as it gets.

Paradoxically, the discovery of new life opportunities can also trigger crises. In such a case, the **crisis curve** will look like this:

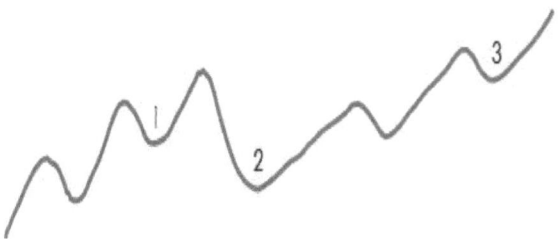

This curve is from psychoanalyst Harald Schjelderup's book The Hidden Man. The ascent in the beginning, at 1, can sometimes be much steeper than in the example. It corresponds to the discovery of new opportunities, to openness, contact, creation – in short, what an adventure it actually is to be human. The steep decline, at 2, is brought about by insight into the enormous difficulties that prevent the realization of these opportunities – personal difficulties and others related to cultural and social conditions, as well as insights into existential data that we previously ignored. One example is the certainty of death. The other and more definitive ascent, at 3, starts when we have "buried" whatever it was we had to give up, such as various illusions, and started to develop our ability to overwin the difficulties.

The Doors between the Rooms

It is interesting to follow the transitions between the spaces in the Matrix through the "doors" between them. We go from CONTENTMENT to CENSORSHIP, either through a hard blow of fate or without even realizing it. Metaphorically speaking, there is no real door, it is more of a trap door. The transition from CENSORSHIP to CONFUSION is through boredom, depression, emptiness, a feeling of "something missing", but what? When you say to yourself: I am censoring, I am actually in CENSORSHIP, then perhaps you have already begun to walk through the door to the Room of Confusion. Figuratively speaking, the door consists of two halves. One half says something like *self-insight* and the other half says *feedback*.

You go through the door to CONFUSION by choosing uncertainty and search (for truth, freedom, self-discovery) and being willing to give up old truths and let things go.

If there were an inscription on the door to INSPIRATION, it would say something about courage and objectivity. And about making decisions. When we know what we want to do, but fear prevents us from doing it; when we see what we realistically need to do but put it off until tomorrow or next year because it is difficult or unpleasant, then we can get stuck in a YES, in conflict and confusion. But at some point, a decision must be made, either by ourselves or by 'circumstances'.

The CONTENTMENT door is probably saying something about the need to compromise. Or that it's okay to harvest the fruits of our work and rest.

Many ongoing processes

It's also possible to go through a mini version of this crisis – for example, in a week, or a day or just a few moments. Perhaps someone is sitting in a group for example, and feeling distracted and bored. The person understands that it is a censorship effect. He or she is holding back an emotion, a thought about what is happening here and now that she is not expressing. The person voices it and notices, perhaps to her surprise, that own discomfort vanished, and he or she may have even influenced others so that the conversation came alive.

Movement between the different rooms is constant and can happen more or less quickly. We can also be in completely different rooms almost simultaneously: at work, in our families, our free time, and among various friends.

The Rooms and the Movements between them

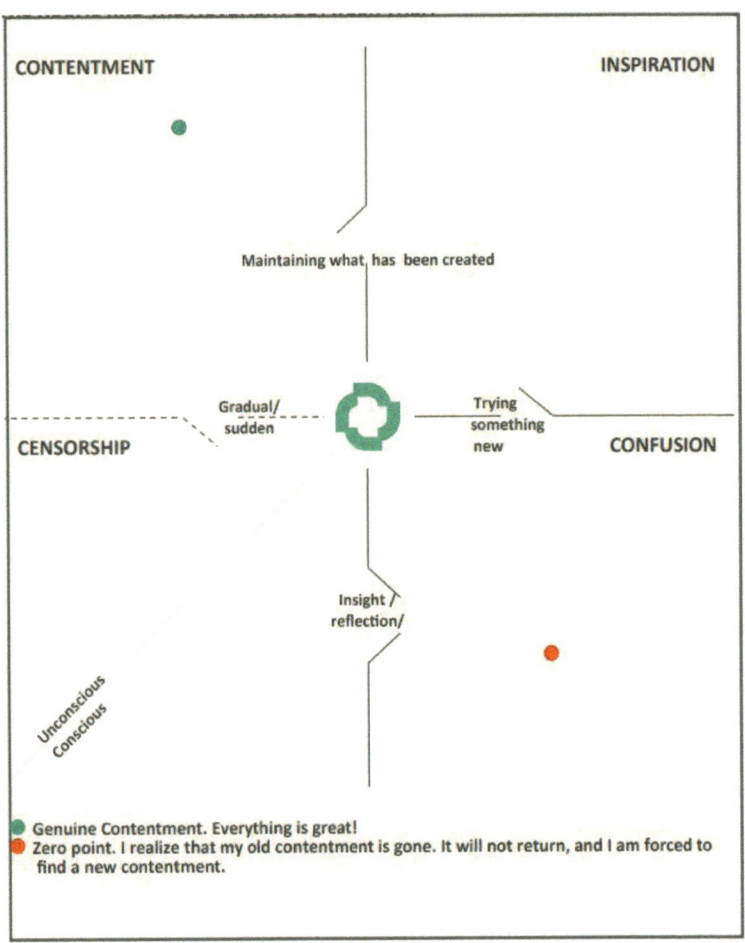

Two types of CENSORSHIP

It is essential to differentiate between two different types of censorship. We can censor unconsciously or consciously. **Unconsciously** is when we censor the truth to ourselves and do not understand that we are censoring. **Consciously** is when we are not actually censoring the truth, we are simply avoiding taking the consequences and acting thereafter.

Our position on the Personal Dialectics scale impacts movements between the doors.

We move constantly among the different rooms, CONTENTMENT, CENSORSHIP, CONFUSION and INSPIRATION. But one's perception of what it is like to be in the various rooms differs depending on where one is on the scale.

If we have many NO answers

Then we need a great deal of Contentment to feel good. But we can also easily find ourselves in Censorship since we often choose to censor when our contentment is threatened. For us, a sense of belonging and community is usually very important. But if this sense of belonging is threatened, we may tend to compromise or keep our opinions to ourselves if they are different in an attempt to avoid being excluded from the community.

If we have many YES answers

Then we need a great deal of Inspiration to feel good. But this also means that we have more confusion since we do not stay put in Contentment but venture into new, unknown situations. As a rule, we have a large need for freedom and to live according to what we feel is right. If we cannot do so, we prefer to leave the community rather than compromise.

People who are to the far left on the dialectic scale, (many NO-Answers) tend to believe that their standpoint is the right one, that "this is how we think in a community". People who are to the far right on the scale, instead perceive that they are quite alone regarding their standpoints. But both perspectives are equally common.

Free Dialectics

If we view the four boxes as a house with four rooms, then happiness may consist of leaving the doors open to allow self-directed movement between the rooms. We can call these free dialectics. Free dialectics assumes an awareness of and understanding for all four attitudes. Free dialectics is desirable on all three levels, within people, between people and in society. One prerequisite for this is that we eliminate the negative perception of confusion, which makes us afraid to enter that room.

Just like it's preferrable that we allow *ourselves* to have a crisis, it is preferrable to consider crises as a natural part of *relationships* between people. A relationship also includes periods of Contentment and adjustment, of Censorship, of Confusion and of creative Inspiration and change.

 Society too must have an "emergency response plan" and a readiness for change. This is where the second meaning of dialectics comes in – as in the art of conversation – since a more direct communication, a creative dialogue between YES and NO respondents is a way to achieve this. An open dialogue can be incredibly potent. In itself, it can be a driving force for societal changes.

2.6 NO and YES – and more of both

Marvin Weisbord, a well-known organizational consultant, summarized the effects of the Four Rooms of Change in one sentence. He said that it is "an incredibly good way to give people the freedom to discover what is happening in the moment". The theory has two decisive effects. The first is that it creates an understanding for what CG Jung refers to as **the magnificent also/and**. We could rephrase this as *both* NO *and* YES, and by extension, more of both.

One example: Here are two facts that appear to contradict each other. We are all special and unique, at the same time, each one of us is simply a regular human being. There is no person exactly like you with your genes and your special life experiences. There has never been anyone exactly like you, nor will there ever be. Your life is an experiment, unique unto you. At the same time, we are all regular human beings and the differences between us are, from another perspective, completely negligeable. You are simply yet another version among millions and millions existing under the same theme: the art of living, the art of being human.

The originality that is perceived as negative, such as the painful feeling of being different, is one of the characteristics of Confusion and conflict. In the same way, the pleasant feeling of commonality, of being basically like others or "just being human" is central to contentment.

NO respondents appear to prioritize commonality and search for roots here. However, this can morph into a trap if they thereby lose contact with their originality, what makes them special.

YES respondents prioritize originality – they strive for a creative expression for that which is special in themselves. This can become a peril if they thereby lose contact with their commonality.

Some people unfortunately exemplify what could be referred to as **the miserable neither/ nor**. They neither manage to fit in nor to achieve a creative life alternative.

The wonderful also/and in this context is knowing that I am both common and unique, and that I look for myself in both directions.

When I claim my commonality more fully, I can express my uniqueness more clearly and inspirationally, and the more I do so, the more satisfied I will feel in my commonality.

Also/ and[4]

more wholehearted acceptance (of the acceptable)	more effective inquisitiveness
more relaxation here and now	bolder dreams in the future
more realistic self-criticism	deeper self-acceptance
broader extroversion	deeper introversion
more simplicity	more complexity
more self-discipline	more initiative
more respect for boundaries	freer pushing of boundaries
more realism	more creativity
greater balance	more openness to change
deeper sense of belonging	stronger individuality
more responsibility	more freedom

For every opposite pair, there are four possible positions. I can feel both realistic and creative. I can be realistic but not creative. I can also be creative but not realistic. And finally, I can be neither creative nor realistic.

I can feel both free and responsible. I can be responsible but not free. I can also be free but not responsible. And I can be neither free nor responsible.

The other effect of the theory is that it affects people's perception of Confusion, which can now be considered a "not too bad state of mind". The power in Inspiration and renewal lies concealed in Confusion and conflict. This is a life phase that "is as natural for our species as breathing" to quote Weisbord again. It "pollinates growth, engagement, creativity, joy, energy and shared commitments".[6]

So far, we have looked at the Four Rooms in each of us. How the Yes/No conflicts work in us as individuals. The great achievement of Claes Janssen is that he connects the Four Rooms to social systems, to teams in organizations, to families, and to society. So, we will have a look at the four rooms in organizations in the next chapter.

2.7. Four Rooms in Organizations

The organization's needs, just as a person's are both

> hard (Being effective)
> and
> soft (Feeling inspired).

This is easy to realize, if we look at the organization in the light of the theory. The effective organization will be high in Contentment, the inspired organization high in Inspiration. In this light, the organization is seen as a person, an analogy which brings alive its "organismic reality". [5]

What does that mean for the different rooms?

The most important prerequisite for being in contentment is having realistic goals for which there is consensus, and which are achieved. A company with sufficient profitability demonstrates that it has adapted to its reality, its market. The personnel will probably have confidence in each other and their management, just like a person in contentment has self-confidence. The atmosphere is relaxed.

A person in censorship shuts themself off from problems. Either the aspects of a situation are not fully understood or they are understood but the person does not take the consequences of what he or she sees. When an organization is in censorship, serious issues such as rumors and gossip are dealt with, but not at official meetings where they should be addressed. There are major information gaps in every direction. The atmosphere is tense, irritating or boring. There are rules and regulations, but they are not well considered and do not work. Risk-taking is not encouraged; doing nothing and avoiding criticism is preferred over trying and risking failure. Tactical considerations are prioritized over quality and personal goals over those of the organization.

A person in confusion is divided by conflicts. An organization in confusion is characterized by a lack of integration. There is a lack of unity in terms of objectives, priorities and goals, or the goals are not reached at all. There are shortcomings in collaboration; the right hand doesn't know what the left hand is doing. There are open conflicts, territorial battles and lack of order. A company where confusion is stronger than contentment is in crisis and knows it.

A person is inspired by their life-concept; a company is inspired by its business concept. An organization in strong inspiration gives its people space to take initiative and for creative ideas. It is characterized by open communication in every direction. Everyone listens to everyone's ideas. The work feels exciting, and the organization is open and flexible.

Groups in the Four Rooms

CONTENTMENT	INSPIRATION
<ul><li>we are satisfied, produce and deliver</li><li>we know what we should do</li><li>we trust each other</li><li>we have control</li><li>we are pleased with the work we do</li><li>we work efficiently</li><li>the members of the team like each other</li><li>working together is uncomplicated</li></ul>	<ul><li>the job is filled with new challenges</li><li>new visions and strategies</li><li>nothing is impossible</li><li>we listen to each other's ideas and bounce them around</li><li>no one wants to go home in the evening.</li></ul>
CENSORSHIP	**CONFUSION**
<ul><li>we have problems, but don't acknowledge them</li><li>we miss external signals</li><li>we are overrun by our competitors</li><li>we feel dissatisfied with what we produce</li><li>we don't listen to each other</li><li>we don't listen to our boss</li><li>mechanical, robotic, unreal</li><li>cynical</li></ul>	<ul><li>we know that we have problems</li><li>we don't know how to solve them</li><li>we have many unanswered questions, who should do what</li><li>who is in charge</li><li>what are our goals</li><li>what do we need to do</li></ul>

Movement of Teams and Organizations

An organization moves slightly differently than a person does. Among other things, this means that Contentment and Inspiration can follow each other. The same applies to Censorship and Confusion.

If Censorship and Confusion increase in a team, it almost always means that Contentment and Inspiration decline. The same applies in the reverse: if Contentment and Inspiration increase, as a rule, Censorship and Confusion decline.

Importance of the different Movements

The difference between the movement of individuals and organizations is important. If you are in a critical situation with the company, it doesn't mean that all people are in censorship. And what plagiarists like House of Change suggest is not useful - on the contrary, it harms the organization.

If you try to get all the people in the room of censorship at the same, which by the way is not possible - what we have outlined before - it has a negative effect on the organization. People who are still in Contentment are still "productive". Some people may already be in Inspiration, and it's good to have people in different rooms to move forward and act.

Gain organizational self-insight and catalyze change

It is possible to work with groups using different instruments Claes Janssen developed. With the Instrument Situational Analysis or Pulsometer leaders and teams can make the present situation describable. Team members have to answer 40 questions (10 for each room) and work directly together with the result. Organizational self-insight and a description of the present situation of the organization is gained. The organizational reality is described as it is collectively felt, experienced, The Four Rooms offers the possibility to describe and deal with the complex emotional situation with four Words without leaving anything significant out. It´s easy – for people to locate themselves in which room they are right now and how the act and as a benefit for the Management it makes the thoughts and feelings transparent- **it delivers a map and a compass.**

These effects are only possible if the common-sense theory made common knowledge before. This is crucial, because by working out the theory together, by understanding the different perspectives on life, a common language, energy and the common willingness to make a change are produced. It catalyzes change and creates action.

The process strengthens **the most decisive factor in workplace satisfaction** – the relative self-determination one has over one´s personal situation.

Doing NOTHING as a consequence of the YES/NO conflicts in Organizations.

Working with Four Rooms de-dramatizes the YES/NO conflicts. Instead of either or thinking which is common and so frequently a dead end, a natural understanding of the already described magnificent both/and will be developed.

Claes Janssen outlined that we are living in a world of conflicts: *"We make one another uncomfortable. The Four Rooms of Change will not change this. But it will make the difficulties easy to understand. To bring up the YES/NO conflict immediately and create a consensus on them- which shows that they are matter we all know, have experienced in depth, in numerous situations-*

seems to "de-dramatize "them more effectively. The conflicts are
shown to be natural, a fact of life- so it´s not strange, but quite
understandable, that we feel uncomfortable together. When we
"agree upon our disagreements, we are forced to take the conse-
quences. All right, we feel uncomfortable – so what? There is a
task to be done." [7]

Doing nothing is no option, lets learn:
Agree to our Disagreements

Claes Janssen wrote this in 2011 and referred to the climate crisis,
for example. The challenges we all face like the climate crises,
wars, Transformations through digital innovations and KI and so
on will not disappear. At the end of the theory section, we want
to reiterate our motivation for this book. Decades of work with
Four Rooms in a wide variety of organizations, schools, institu-
tions, and cultures have shown that it helps individuals **to deal
with development and change** and **the commonsense** theory
can be a pragmatic catalyst for creating more **common spirit**.

Four Rooms

in practice

3. Four Rooms in practice

This chapter contains practical examples carried out by different Certified Users in different countries and continents and with different target groups - students, masters, managers and athletes. The aim is to show that Four Rooms can be used in a wide variety of contexts. The Certified Users invite to delve into their respective development processes. They share their reflections on how helpful the respective participants found Four Rooms, where there were obstacles and also how they as Consultants, Leaders or Coaches feel while using the Four Rooms.

3.1 So, I'm still in the Censorship! Clarifying coaching goals

Dr. Doris Yuan

This coaching case is about how I helped the coachee use the Four Rooms of Change to gain insight into her true emotional state in different relationships in the face of change at work, ultimately clarifying the coaching goals.

Insights during Coaching

For those coachees who take actions quickly, coaches need to have the courage to press the 'pause' button and accompany them to 'see' what the motivation behind the fast action is.

Sometimes fast action is just a way to 'avoid' a hidden sense of vulnerability. They tend to act out of the anxiety they feel when they are overwhelmed by their own or other people's emotions. They simply close their eyes and block out their emotions. However, this is more of a reckless 'beating around the bush' approach than a real move forward through the zero point.

Client

The Coachee is a lady who is working for an American company in China as a Finance Manager. The company arranged a six-month coaching program for her to improve her leadership skills. She is very smart and rational, with high action power. During the coaching process in the past four months, she has gained a lot of insights and actions, and her leadership improvement has been recognised by her boss and colleagues.

Coaching process

Coachee: In this coaching session, I would like to ask you to help me broaden my view a bit more, in the face of the current operational difficulties, to see what other things we can do in the finance team.

Doris: What has happened to make you bring this topic?

Coachee: The market conditions in our industry have actually been getting worse since the end of 2023. Especially in the last three months, our sales have dropped dramatically, and with all the costs increasing in the operation, the company has been making huge losses. At last week's management team meeting the general manager very suddenly proposed two improvements: firstly, price increases for some product lines; and secondly, salary reductions for all staff. He said this was a suggestion given by our finance department after analysing the situation. I agree to reduce costs and increase efficiency, but whether the current bad market environment allows us to raise prices? Will a full payroll cut force out some high-value employees? How can all these be proposed without prior justification? I've been mulling over this for the last few days and have come up with some ideas, but I don't think they are enough, and my head is dopey sometimes.

So, I'd like to ask you to help me broaden my mind and see if there's a better way.

Doris: I'm sorry to hear the bad news. You just mentioned the word 'dopey', are you unwell?

Coachee: I don't have any physical problems, but I just feel like my brain is a mess, I can't think clearly, and I can't concentrate for long periods of time. How can I put it, it's like not sleeping well at night and then waking up in the morning with a foggy head.

Doris: How has your sleep been lately?

Coachee: Not too bad. Well, not too good actually. I've been having dreams at night during these days, some weird ones, but I can't remember what they were about. I wake up tired every morning though, but I'm sure it's not a physical problem.

Doris: Another thing I'm curious about regarding your narrative above is how you felt when the GM wanted to make you a scapegoat at the management meeting.

Coachee: Feelings huh? ...... (silence). Well, there was a bit of shock and anger. But who made him the GM! And he was kind of nice to me in the past. Being a subordinate is inherently a scapegoat for the leader!

Doris: Do you remember the Four Rooms of Change theory we've talked about and used before? What would you discover if you used this theory to help you become aware of your emotional state in that moment again?

Coachee: I was in the room of Contentment before the meeting, and then after my boss made two suggestions in the meeting, I 'whooshed' into the room of Censorship. I was a little angry, but I knew the boss must have his points; and I had to recognise the fact that the employee was the boss's 'scapegoat', so I went into the room of Confusion and started thinking about how to find a way out. That was it!

Doris: You sounded very strong when you said 'the employee is the scapegoat for bosses. Do you notice that?

Coachee: Is it? Maybe! But the most important thing is to find a solution, and I don't want people to actually get a pay cut.

Doris: What kind of situation would you face if people did get a pay cut?

Coachee: Well ...... I would be blamed by everyone; in fact, a lot of people are blaming me behind my back now.

Doris: Do these accusations make you feel pain? Are there any other consequences that make you feel pain or fear?

Coachee: It's definitely painful! I don't want that to happen because it would be painful! So back to my topic of finding solutions.

Doris: I hear you're anxious, but in the Four Rooms of Change, we have to get past zero-point to really move forward. Have you found your zero point yet?

Coachee: The zero point means that I can't go back to my former contentment, and I must accept it. I know I have to!

Doris: Where do you accept you can't go back?

Coachee: Can't go back to the easy days like before when the market was good.

Doris: Do you remember that tall building in the Four Rooms of Change? We can also be in completely different rooms when we're in different situations or relationships, like at work, in our families, in our free time, with different friends, etc. It's as if we have a tall building within us, and when faced with different situations or relationships, our emotions are in different rooms on different floors. In your story today, there is your relationship with your GM, your relationship with your job, the situation where you faced accusations from your colleagues at work, and so on. Can we start by looking at which room your relationship with your boss is in?

Coachee:...... (silence). Relationship with my boss......., that's one hasn't really crossed my mind.

Doris: You mentioned before that he was kind of nice to you, so when he shirked his responsibilities to you, you didn't say anything even though you were angry. Did you communicate with him after that meeting? Any form of communication and on any topic. What was your state of mind when you communicated with him?

Coachee: There definitely must be communication, after all, I am the finance manager, and he is the GM. But it seems that I am a bit reluctant to communicate with him, and I seem to be in a hurry when communicating. This morning at the meeting, he also asked me, 'It seems recently you did not rest well? Why do you feel very angry and look tired?

Doris: So, about your relationship with your boss, where will you position yourself in the Four Rooms?

Coachee: That's kind of hard! I haven't really thought about my relationship with my boss in the past, it's just a working relationship, and he kind of valued me and gave me the opportunity to be promoted to this position and gave me the opportunity to be coached. So, I think I should be worthy of his respect and trust. So, I've always been supportive of his decisions at work, and I've always been determined to carry them out. Even till now! It seems like it should always be in the room of contentment for my relationship with my boss, right?

Doris: In the last sentence you used a question rather than an affirmation, and you used the word 'should' twice. What does all this mean?

Coachee: Like that? I didn't even notice. What does all this mean? ...... (silence) It seems that my relationship with my boss is not as harmonious as I thought! Before, I mean before that meeting, from my point of view, I was happy with that hierarchical relationship. But when he shirked his responsibilities on me in that meeting, I got angry at him, so I kind of avoided communicating with him in depth. Does this mean that in my relationship with my boss, I'm in the room of Censorship?

Doris: Indeed! Earlier you mentioned that you have very strange dreams, don't really want to communicate with your boss, tend to rush when communicating, etc. All these behaviours are indicative of what you're running away from, what you don't want to look at, what you don't want to face. So, the important thing is what are you avoiding? What are the realities that you don't want to face?

Coachee: Good question! I never thought about that, what am I running away from? What am I not willing to face? That's a huge question.

Doris: Yeah, do you remember we talked earlier about how leadership is not just about leading subordinates, but also managing superiors. That's when I saw a pattern with you - avoiding opposing authority, even when they're wrong. To keep the harmony relationship with those authorities, you close your eyes, pretend not seeing your uncomfortable feeling. That topic jumped out at me again today, so should we dig deeper about this pattern today?

Coachee: Yes, I also think this topic is much more valuable than my former one, and I want to explore more why I have the pattern of avoiding opposition to authority. I also want to explore what I run away from in my work with bosses and how to change this pattern.

My Reflection:

1. The ´Tall Building` of the Four Rooms of Change theory helps us to disaggregate emotions, rather than generalizing about satisfaction or dissatisfaction, or misplacing emotions about one relationship onto another. This distinction is important and helpful in helping the coachee to clarify the emotions facing different situations.
2. Stopping and digging deeper in the room of Censorship can help the coachee to see many of his/her underlying automatic patterns, and this kind of digging can lead to more radical changes.
3. For this highly coachable coachee, perhaps I could go more directly to the point and give her direct feedback on her relationship with her boss, instead of circling around for clarification.
4. The subsequent exploration of automatic patterns used the Four Rooms of Change and Psychodynamics tools. This combination made the coachee's exploration more tangible.

3.2 Integration of Four Rooms in Leadership Programs in the Production area.

Jens Witte

The often-underestimated leadership role in production

The role of a leader in production is particularly challenging and often underestimated. The work is highly technical and characterized by metrics and transparency. Managers often have to lead large teams of 30 to 150 people with different values, languages, religions, and cultures. At the same time, they must be very transparent about their performance, because it is all about numbers, quantity and quality. This transparency extends to the minute-by-minute scheduling of breaks, which is often not the case in other areas.

A big part of the challenge is that managers in production are highly controlled from the outside and must be very reactive, especially during shift work. When I ask managers what they consider to be the real highlights of their daily management work, the top three answers are always: when everything runs smoothly and there is no chaos.

The development into leadership responsibility can be supported by mentoring and training, but if I have people sitting in a seminar who say, "It's great that I'm learning this, but I'm not allowed to apply it, or my boss doesn't want me to talk to my people, or I'm not involved in challenging management decisions," then mentoring and training are of little use. It is important that not only the new managers but also their superiors are involved, and the following practical example shows how this can be supported: A group of managers is working together to address the problem of excessive cell phone use by employees. During a lengthy discussion in a training group of 12 people, it became clear that there were different opinions about how long and in what situations cell phones should be used. Other questions that arose were

What could a policy look like? How can this be implemented now?

How do you communicate this? The group decided to work on this issue in parallel with the learning journey to develop and implement rules. This involved the environment, their own managers, HR and the works council, as well as a joint review of the outdated company agreement, which completely prohibited the wearing of cameras and led to immediate dismissal. The end of the Learning Journey was chosen so that the last module of support took place after the conclusion of a company agreement on this topic, in order to ensure a common understanding and to talk about the discussions with the employees. Such practical projects, integrated into learning journeys, help to solve concrete problems and support managers in their development and in taking on more responsibility. In summary, training and support in production areas must be extremely practical.

Janssen's model - can the Four Rooms be used in production?

When I did a Four Rooms of Change certification in 2018, I thought Oh God, this doesn't work on the shop floor and asked myself whether it was too abstract for production areas.

When I come round the corner with questions such as what is the meaning of life? Is that too far removed from practice and I thought OK, that's an exciting field, but it's probably not the right thing for the production sector, which wants to deal with something tangible.

I was very sceptical as to whether it would fit together, but I still wanted to try it out. Now I've done the introduction - the development of the Four Rooms of Change with more than 70 groups and **it works brilliantly**!

It's always inspiring to see how intensively the participants get involved and how much they can do with it. The managers really realise what the social structure in their teams is like and that there is a lot of interpersonal interaction. They think a lot about how to minimise conflict and how to improve the atmosphere.

Four Rooms helps them a lot because it is a clear model that can be understood quickly and the path through the changes is a clear process. It even fits very well in the production area. It connects very well with the participants because they are used to processes and can understand the clarity of the model and the process through the rooms very well. Based on their own experience, they confirm the process and perceive it as logical. They describe when someone is doing well and when they are not. Where is my counterpart now? Is he still in denial or already in confusion? The intense preoccupation with the Four Rooms can also be seen in the fact that the names of the rooms are considered. This happened, for example, with the name of the Room of Denial. One group insisted on calling it the Room of Unconscious and Conscious Self-mockery. This is a slightly different word, but it gets to the heart of the matter. It reflects directly on one's own experience of discussion situations, e.g. under the following question "What is my employee striving for more, the area of satisfaction or the area of inspiration?" The groups discuss intensively that as a manager you have to react differently depending on in which room someone is. From the participants' point of view, this is logical, and a lot of work is done with logic on the shop floor.

Transfer to everyday life

In learning journeys in which the group is accompanied over a longer period of time with face-to-face training, virtual small group meetings and, if possible, coaching sessions, I make the introduction at the beginning of the learning journey in order to use the Four Rooms as a basic model again and again in the training sessions and, above all, in everyday life. The depth and support of the model becomes much stronger the longer you work with it.

As already mentioned, the practical orientation is very important. Interestingly, I often find that the Four Rooms find their way into everyday life even without an assignment between training days. Participants explain it at home and describe how they have reacted. The tangibility and the simple wording make it possible. Nevertheless, there are also critical comments during the training. I'm now looking forward to hearing the participants say

OK, Jens this is completely logical, but what am I supposed to do with it now, so we don't say here's my coke, it's finished, when I'm thirsty I'll fill it up again.

Then I drink it again and I'm satisfied until I'm thirsty again? It's the same process, I do it anyway. Why does knowing the process help me now?

It's always a great discussion in the group when suddenly the second and third person come in and say, "*Well, let's say you have an employee who's settled in well, who's doing a good job, but who likes to take more breaks than others. Is he comfortable with that, even if he feels like he's dancing around a little bit and you're letting him do that? But somehow, as a manager, you get upset about it, and so do other colleagues.*"

Then you have to react. Then it helps to know where you stand and what you want to change. Where is the employee, is he aware of the consequences of his actions, is he in denial, or do I have to set clear boundaries and point out the consequences?

Another example that was discussed is that it makes a difference if you approach someone who has been doing almost the same thing for 20 years, so they don't immediately shout *hurray* at the introduction of a new machine, for example. Satisfaction, stability and security are important to them, so it doesn't make sense to focus on the great machine and what it can do, but rather on how it secures their job in the long term and how they can no longer do the same thing but remain in the same working environment - in other words, what has a stabilizing effect and provides security. And that's what people start to understand and grasp, that leadership means that I have to treat people differently and to stay with the example, the next employee is in the room of inspiration, he is excited about the introduction of the new machine, he has other questions and needs.

That's when it clicks. And you get statements like:

Ah exciting no wonder I can't win my colleague over to this if I spray him with my enthusiasm and he finds it rather stupid.

During the learning journey, participants come back with many more specific use cases where they have used the Four Rooms as a tool to supplement their traditional leadership behaviour in specific conversations with their employees. Classically, this means that they have to talk to employees about misconduct, e.g. if there is too much waste, the conversation often goes something like this:

Kalle, you shouldn't make so much waste, and then he says yes, I'm sorry, and that's it.

The discussion about misbehaviour is still there, but it has a different structure and becomes more individual. You think about it beforehand and change the conversation depending on the room in which you see the employee. Is the employee unaware that he is producing waste, does he not care, or does he simply not know what needs to be changed? Is it someone who is looking for satisfaction and stability, or rather inspiration, i.e. someone who thinks he is improving the process and doing the right thing?

Supplement traditional leadership behaviours

With this preliminary analysis, they can supplement their traditional leadership behaviours and respond more individually to employees to ultimately bring about the desired change in behaviour.

Even during trainings or workshops, there are "aha" moments that are enough for some people to make a very important decision. One of my most memorable experiences was a workshop with a management team at a manufacturing site that was facing existential challenges. The site was on the verge of collapse, and the team was made up of what the site manager considered to be very unique individuals. The management team went through the introduction together, and in subsequent positioning exercises in four rooms, talked in depth about how they were dealing with the situation. This gave them the space to address everything openly and then take further steps to improve the situation.

And the best part was when the site manager took me aside late after the workshop and said:

Before the workshop, I was quite clear that I wanted to quit and that I was the wrong person. After this workshop and working with Four Rooms, I've become more aware of a lot of things, and I now have a clear plan on how I can move this site forward. I'm staying here.

A look at a prejudice: The willingness to change in manufacturing is low

It is often said that the willingness and ability to change is lower in manufacturing than in other areas.

This is not my experience. I see the same distribution of both views as in other groups. People from all areas think that there are more people who are looking for stability and security and a place of contentment.

There is a perception that this is 80% of society, that this is the majority, and that there is only a minority of 20% for whom the meaning of their actions and doing the right thing is important. This is a fallacy, as Claes Janssen's research has confirmed. It's a 50/50 split, and that's exactly what I experience in production areas.

What surprised me was that production managers often start by working on themselves. Change starts with me -it is observable. They don't wait to look at others first. In learning journeys, we start with the introduction and the following statements emerge:

OK, if I'm unhappy with something, I must do something - I can't always just say my bosses have to do something, so I have to get into my own framework of action when I discover myself in the Room of Censorship.

Then I just have to do something.

You notice when your bosses don't solve problems and you're unhappy with the situation. *Then I probably must push the issue of vacation planning, for example, even though I'm only responsible for one shift. Whether or not radio is allowed in production needs to be clarified.*

They reflect that if I don't resolve it, I'm in denial or confused about the situation. I'm always happy when people see that for themselves and say, hey cool, I just need to be more assertive in my leadership, which historically hasn't always been the case in the production areas.

In summary, I have experienced in my more than 70 groups that Four Rooms works very well in production areas. It is a logical tool for everyday life.

It has also helped me to question my own stereotypes, and if someone had told me beforehand that I would be discussing the meaning of life with shift supervisors, I would have said that they definitely wouldn't be doing this psychobabble. But this was only possible through the process of the group working out the theory together.

I'm also always happy to see how Four Rooms strengthens managers, also in terms of taking responsibility for their own actions.

In my opinion, Four Rooms and leadership in production go very well together, now that I have been able to translate the way we work it out for myself. Even though I do the Four Rooms several times a month with different groups, I never get bored. I learn something new from the group every time, and that keeps me motivated.

3.3. Building Organizational Resilience with Four Rooms

Dr. Angelika Schrand

The concept of organizational resilience in the corporate world is particularly relevant in times of constant change and uncertainty. Organizations must be able to adapt to crises and new circumstances, survive disruptions and recover quickly. At CONTUR, we have experienced some turbulent times and even disruptive changes in our business over the past few years. We are a training and consulting company for leadership, strategy, change, project management, assessment solutions and sustainability. With around 60 employees and 150 network partners, we operate internationally from Germany, China and Mexico.

The pace of change in the education market has accelerated significantly during the Covid phase. The rapid growth of virtual work, platforms and tools, the development of digital academies and competition from other sectors are presenting us with enormous challenges. On top of this, our customers are also undergoing transformation processes in different ways depending on the industry, and the entire economy is in crisis, which is directly reflected in reduced spending on human resources development and even the suspension of all training that is not legally required. In this chapter, I would like to show how working with Four Rooms has made us more resilient in overcoming these crises.

Core elements that are frequently mentioned in publications on organizational resilience are the ability to adapt quickly and effectively to change, the resilience to withstand and recover from setbacks, the anticipation and preparation for potential threats and the willingness to learn. To develop organizational resilience, a culture of openness, trust and innovation is required.

In 2018, I qualified as a Four Rooms of Change Certified User in Sweden. Since then, we have certified other colleagues, and all employees at CONTUR have participated in the introduction so that we all have a common understanding. We have used Four Rooms as a feedback format in both face-to-face and virtual events. At the beginning of 2019, we held a joint strategy workshop in person and worked on the strategic goals and specific objectives for 2019. We have had a very successful year financially. At the end of the workshop, when we asked everyone to position themselves in the four Rooms to see how they felt about our direction, we got an interesting picture. Many were in the contentment and inspiration room, but some were also in the Censorship room. It was very helpful to share why there were such different perspectives on the topic, as some already saw threats to our business and feared that we were not preparing enough. This perspective helped us a lot because it allowed us to work more consistently on innovation.

With other feedback methods, this might have been expressed, but then it takes a lot of courage to make critical comments. In addition, the classification of others is different. Critical comments are not dismissed as nagging, resistance or pessimism, but are immediately transformed into a "wanting to understand" with the question - what is it that brings you into the Room of Censorship or confusion. It makes you more capable of speaking and makes it easier to address emotions within a structured framework. The consistent use of Four Rooms as a "position-fixing or feedback tool" has resulted in a different, more constructive culture of discussion and greater understanding of different points of view.

We have intensified the use of Four Rooms since 2022. As part of our strategic focus on becoming a sustainable company, we considered how we could also measure the social pillar of sustainability as part of the DNK (German Sustainability Report). Under the title "Creating good and healthy working conditions", we used another Four Rooms tool, the Pulsometer (situation analysis). It consists of 40 questions that show at the organizational level how strong Contentment and Inspiration are or whether the corporate culture tends to lead to Censorship or Confusion and thus to frustration, feelings of powerlessness, resignation or uncertainty - in other words, to conditions that are not conducive to productivity and the ability to innovate. The questions and statements are rated on a scale of 1 to 10, with the higher the score for Contentment and Inspiration, the more positive. Examples of questions in these areas are

- We have clear tasks at CONTUR, we know what we have to do and we feel good about it.
- The meetings deal with important issues effectively without becoming impersonal and boring.
- In CONTUR we trust each other.

Statements about the Rooms of Censorship and Confusion are for example:

- There are strong tensions in CONTUR that are almost never openly visible.
- Many in CONTUR are reluctant to speak their minds.
- " That's not possible" is often heard in CONTUR.
- Smaller scores are better in the lower rooms, because if agreement with the statements is low, in the example "Many in CONTUR are reluctant to speak their minds this means that it is not perceived that way."

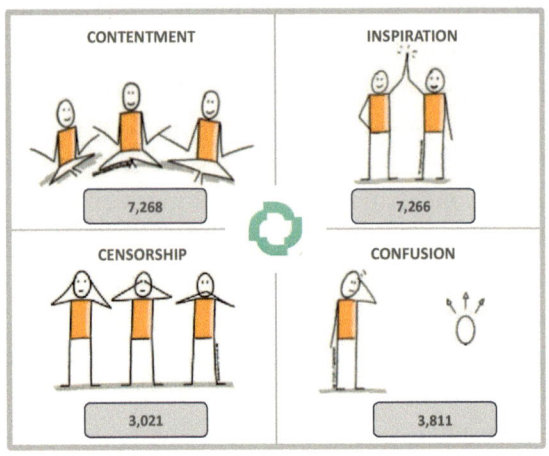

The survey was conducted anonymously on two levels. On the one hand, all employees were able to evaluate CONTUR and on the other hand their own team. We presented the overall results to all employees in virtual meetings and worked on them together. The respective team leaders analyzed the team results directly with the team and worked on specific improvements. For the DNK report, we used the Well Being Index and set ourselves a target. In 2022 the Wellbeing Index was 3.85. We set a target of 4.5. In March 2023, we reached 4.58. In particular, the Contentment and Inspiration scores went up, and what we were particularly pleased about was that we were able to reduce the Censorship score to 2.56.

But what does that mean? When there are high scores in the Room of Censorship, unconscious or conscious, it indicates that the need for change is not seen or agreed upon. For example, you might hear: *In the past everything was better. We don't have a need for what they have in mind up on the Top Management level. We will go through this change project and then everything will be the same.* We were able to reduce that thinking through our work together. The decisive factor here is what we have worked on it in common.

In contrast to other employee surveys, the results are worked on directly with those affected. And the key was not the processing in the whole group, but the joint analysis and reflection in the teams.

In addition to the overall results, it is important to look at the distribution of responses. For example, if there is a high distribution in the question: "Many in CONTUR are reluctant to speak their mind", this shows a different perception of the situation. And at those points the discussions become more intense. As one team leader said: *I was very skeptical whether this would achieve anything, but by sharing different perceptions we managed to get to the heart of the matter and not just derive superficial measures.*

We continue to do the surveys, meanwhile it is much shorter and usually it is done as part of the regular team meetings. We see volatility in the results, and that's a good thing. It is not only a tool for good times, but it should also be transparent about where we are in stormy times.

The results are transparent to everyone, and this minimizing the influence of negative opinion leaders. Instead of a few loud voices dominating, everyone is heard and noticed, which in turn strengthens the well-being of each individual employee.

Have we become more resilient? Yes, we have. We have succeeded in strengthening a culture of openness and trust. This is reflected in the consistently positive response to the question

    - We trust each other at CONTUR

The openness, which is necessary for a resilient corporate culture is underlined by the consistently positive assessment of the statement

> - It is easy to bring in your own ideas and suggestions because others listen and encourage you.

We have overcome all setbacks so far, and one of the keys to this is trusting cooperation within the management team. We have noticed that we are sometimes very far apart on the dialectical scale as we found out with the Personal Dialectics Instrument (see Chapter 2.) On the one hand, there are those who tend to be No answerers, for whom stability, security, conformity to norms, and belonging are important, and on the other hand there are those who tend to be Yes answerers, who want to do the right thing now and in the future, who question whether it makes sense, and who initiate new ideas.

This is very evident when making decisions and we respect and use the different points of view as a strength, even if it is not always pleasant for the other side. In such situations, the quote from Claes Janssen *Agree to your disagreements* often comes to mind.

The Four Rooms language has become a common language and changes our behavior in everyday life. It not only allows us to deal with each other in a more conflict-free manner, but also in a more relaxed and humorous way. And laughing together is not an official criterion for resilience, but it has helped us to get through crises together.

3.4. Generate an open dialogue in a Chinese Start-Up Management Team

Dr. Doris Yuan

The Four Rooms of Change theory and its models and tools are the ones I have studied and applied the most these years, not only in my work but also in my life. Now, I would like to share a case study in which I used the tools – the Introduction and the Pulsometer (Situational Analysis) from the Four Rooms of Change theory to help a Chinese startup management team generate dialogue and find ideas and define actions for team synergy.

Project Background:

At the end of one of The Four Rooms of Change Introduction sharing events, one of the participants asked if he could ask me to do a Four Rooms of Change sharing for his team. He is the GM of the Start-Up Company, and he describes the company and the initial situation:

"Our company is a startup that combines composite material research and development and sales, it was established less than two years ago. There are 21 people in total in the company, and there are seven people in the management team. They say it's the management team, but in reality, they all have to do detail work too."

The organization is a lean structure.

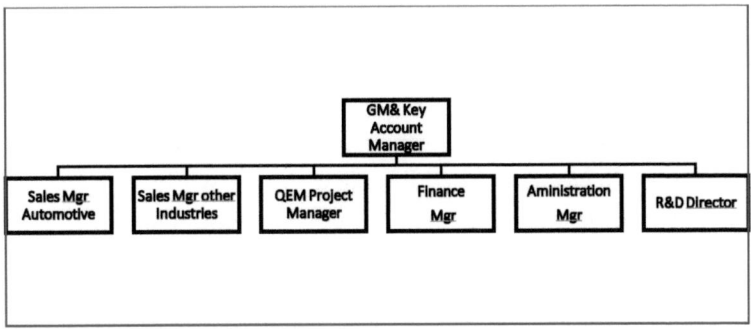

Together with the R&D Directors they created the idea for the company. The R&D Director has technical knowledge of the material- product, which needed to be converted into production, and he had some connections in materials sales, so they decided to make a company to convert those results. They are both shareholders and managers in the team, but he as the GM is basically taking the role of management. The production has been outsourced.

Typical problems arise - on the one hand the customer needs and on the other the hand working with an outsourced partner, which makes it not easier to deliver the products on time and quality.

The initial situation: reflected by the GM:

The GM explains: *I'm tired of serving customers all day and night, but also managing these little things, really exhausted. As a result, I sometimes get angry and make everyone unhappy. After listening to your sharing of the Four Rooms of Change just now, I realized that I didn't recognize that I might be in the censorship room when I was dealing with certain issues, and I didn't want to listen to my colleagues' reasons when I was in the room of confusion. And my colleagues, I guess, some of them who are straight will argue with me directly, but some of them who are sulky, will just wimp out and don't say anything when I get angry. They are also, out of sync with each other on some things, causing inefficiency in the team* ".

The expectations of the GM:

The expectations to do the Introduction with the whole Management Team were: That all members build up awareness and knowledge of themselves and their emotions as I do. He reflects himself as a No Person- and said: *"Now I know I'm a more No person, and I don ' t like intransparency and confusion, but they don't know it yet!"*

The recommendation from my side was that the Introduction is only the first step, and it makes sense to use the Situational Analysis with the Pulsometer to work together as a team on improvements.

Typically for a Chinese start-up entrepreneur ´ s thinking is, not to invest too much time in trainings, they want to see short time results. But after a period of reconsideration, the GM agreed.

The Workshop and the Role as a Facilitator

At the beginning of the workshop, the GM said to everyone in a very short but firm tone, *"I've made up my mind when I asked teacher Yuan to come and give us a training session. It's the end of the year and we're all quite busy, so it's not easy to arrange a whole day of training. But since we're here, let's participate properly, and I hope everyone gets something out of it!"*

I wanted to explain that it wasn't training, but it would make the GM feel humiliated. So, I pointed to the agenda of the day and explained, *"I'm glad to have the opportunity to share some of my insights with you. We'll be learning some new tools today, but more importantly I'll be here to guide and facilitate a session with you using this tool to explore how your team can collaborate and cooperate more effectively."*

As I finished the introduction of the agenda, the Sales Manager quickly said, *"Finally, a time for all of us to sit down together."* I made a note of this statement as I felt it seemed to express a need that was being ignored in this team.

Chinese culture emphasizes introversion and reserve: how to connect and make emotions visible with the Four Rooms

They created the Four Rooms of Change Theory together according to the Introduction Process and in this session, I asked them to close their eyes to experience their feelings and emotions in different situations when I read those words. This was difficult for a few of the male participants, except for the GM. He had already experienced this step when he participated in my previous sharing, but the other men obviously needed some time to experience their feelings. This situation is relatively common in China. Chinese culture emphasizes introversion and reserve, and Chinese men are proud of not showing their emotions in public. For them to be able to experience how they feel in different situations, I read the words that I collected in each quadrant in the previous session while letting them feel their body's reaction. In this way, slowly, they were able to write down one or two words for their feelings. In the pair discussion session, I purposely paired up male and female colleagues so that the men produced more feelings with their female colleagues. When the collection of words was completed, the Sales Manager said that they were usually so busy that the word "feeling" was a bit of a luxury for them in a startup.

Reflections on the Movement and the Two Approaches

As I talked about how we move through the rooms, how our emotions flow through the four rooms as things unfold or situations change, several participants expressed "understood" and " confusion" alternatively.

But when I put up the flip chart explaining the two different approaches to life, everyone breathed a sigh of relief, leaned back in a state of "I see," and then began to look at how many Yes and No they chose.

The first discussion began with the following questions: Do we mainly tend towards NO - are we really ourselves at work? A statement from the GM- *like now you know how to behave at this point* was not helpful. Because I think it will not fit in at this moment to deepen our reflection, we have instead taken the step to the organizational level.

The organizational Four Rooms of Change

I then asked them to consider whether the Four Rooms of Change could be applicable to organizations and teams. All of them answered in unison, "Definitely". As we discussed how the organization performed in the different rooms, everyone came out of silence and reengaged in the discussion.

We quickly worked out a list of how the organization behaved in each room, but when I asked everyone to think about what behavior they saw in their own team, there was silence. I asked everyone to stand in front of this flipchart and go through each behavior. But they kept silent. To break the silence, I asked the GM to vote first. He voted for "insufficient motivation to innovate". Seeing that the GM had voted, others gave their choices: happy, go for it, just do it, complain, ambivalence, and spending money with fear. Except for one person, whose choice was in the contentment room, three team members chose the words in the inspiration room, and three chose the words in the self-censorship room.

I asked the group, *"Is this result consistent with what you thought it would be?"* The GM did not speak this time but frowned at the flip chart. Obviously, the result was not what he expected. The Sales Manager spoke first: *"It's quite consistent! In our company, it's true that everyone can do our work, of course, it's always hard to avoid conflicts and complaints in the process. However, in our company, I'm still quite happy."*

I looked at the other team members and asked, *"Anyone else want to share your thoughts?"*

The finance manager raised her hand and said, *"I don't think that's very consistent. Since when have we been cautious about spending money? I feel like I spend a lot every month when I make payments! No one thinks about whether I have money in this wallet to make payments when they're asking for expenses! "*

The finance manager's comment seemed to put a "!", stopping the discussion.

"Thank you, for sharing!" I thought it would be good for everyone to take a lunch break. So that I could bring in the Pulsometer and catch up from these two different perspectives in the afternoon. *"Just now we had some colleagues who felt that everyone's choices on the flipchart were aligned with the current state of the team, and some colleagues who felt that they were not. It looks like we need more time to dig a little deeper into why the differences are there. What exactly is the difference? What can we do*

to come to an agreement on the team's perceptions. Please think about these questions during lunch and take a break!"

Lunch & Break

During lunch, everyone sits around a large round table, which is typical of Chinese team-building culture - eating to bond. The GM was keen to bring the conversation back to what we had been discussing, but it was clear that the team members weren't buying it and were no longer talking enthusiastically. Once again, I could feel that the team's energy was stuck. To lighten the mood, the R&D Director jumped in and tried to create a more relaxed environment. It was a typical Chinese startup management team: a strong leader, a deputy who bridges the gap between leader and team members, a loyal finance manager, and a slick sales and other follower in support departments.

This kind of observation was helpful because I couldn't do in-depth interviews in the pre-workshop period, so this observation opportunity gave me a chance to get to know this team better and get some clues for the afternoon work.

The introduction of the Pulsometer (Situational Analysis)

Back in the meeting room, I gathered everyone in front of the flipchart again, reviewed the discussion we had before lunch, and then asked everyone *"Is there anything you would like to say about this difference?"*

"Because we stand on a different perspective, after all, sales and finance position are different!" one said. Another remark was: *"People and people are also different! Just like what Teacher Yuan said in the morning, some people have more Yes, and some people have more No. They will have different feelings and opinions about the same thing."*

I added: *"Yes, this difference is caused both by the difference in the positions held and the different perspectives from which one looks at the problem. Teams are made up of different people, each one with their own characteristics and positions, so there will always be many different voices in the team. But could we voice out these different opinions in the past? Do we have the opportunity and patience to hear these different voices in our busy work? And what do different voices mean to the team? Risk or opportunity?"* I threw out another series of questions.

Everyone looked at each other when they heard these questions and waited for me to say what I was going to say.

"I'm going to guide you through the process of unlocking another tool based on the Four Rooms of Change Theory, which is a great tool for facilitating team dialogue. Now please return to your seats to complete the 40 questions about your team."

When the questions were answered and the statistics were calculated and presented on the flipchart, everyone was still a little unsure but felt that their team's Inspiration Room score was low. I explained that this result couldn't be determined simply by looking at the score numbers, but by looking at the distribution of each team member's score. Just like our pre-lunch discussion, there were two views on the same issue. This was an opportunity for us to see and understand that there were differences in everyone's thoughts on the issue. So, one of the other things we would do was to look at the distribution of everyone's answers.

Analysis: What is behind the numbers

As expected, looking at the distribution brought us all a more visual presentation of the team's ideas. Before I could say anything, the participants were pointing to some of the questions where the answers were spread out and discussing them in whispers.

"Now I'm going to take you on a deeper exploration of the distribution. During this process I will invite you to share your thoughts as you answer the questions. As your colleague shares, others can recognize whether all of you have the same understanding of the questions, furthermore, to understand why there is a difference by observing how this peer thinks. At the same time, you can gain better insight by seeing how your group's members have answered the questions and what that means for your teams' climate. Let's move on to see how the answers are distributed" I say this as I put the facilitation questions on the flipchart.

The first question in the Contentment room gave me a great opportunity to facilitate conversation. There were 3 people who disagreed with the statement - **Most things are good enough as they are**-, and 3 agreed and 1 didn't know. I invited the partners who had chosen to disagree on this question to share their thoughts and then invited the partners who had chosen to agree and don't know to share their thoughts as well. This was a dialogue process in which the GM, who chose to disagree (0 points), expressed his dissatisfaction and his feeling that everyone could have done better. The partner who chose to agree said that everyone was doing a good job under the current conditions, even 110%. Yet, they also complained that some work they had done was not always seen. The GM was clearly surprised to hear this, saying that he felt he had acknowledged everyone's contribution, but he had not realized that nearly half of the team members felt that they were not seen to be doing things.

To avoid the dialogue getting stocked down again, I guided them to see that the most important thing in this session was that everyone's ideas were expressed and heard, and that everyone was both an expresser and a listener. So, in the process of expression and listening, first do not rush to judge and to find a solution, we were now in the analysis, that was, to let the problem be presented and then be recorded on the flipchart. There would be a session later to lead them to look for solutions.

When we came to the first question in the censorship room, the GM and the R&D Director were faced with a huge challenge. The question was: **At present the serious problems within our group are talked about in corridors, not in meetings.** Both chose to disagree, while others chose to agree. Both looked at the other members of the team and asked sincerely, *"What are the issues that can't be discussed in public? Why does it have to be discussed privately?"*

After everyone was silent for a few seconds, the finance manager broke the silence. *"The problem of untimely receivable returns has been told to you several times, but it hasn't been solved! You hold the company's key customers, accounting for more than half of the sales. Some of these key customers have a 90-day payment period, and occasionally maybe four or five months before the money comes into our account. So sometimes I really can't find money to pay for some purchase. This is something I can't advertise publicly, right?"*

"Yes, yes, I totally agree with the finance manager. There is no money in the company account, so the finance manager can't pay for outsourcing, thus, I cannot ask the factories to prioritize the production of our products. You still count me as a wimp every time, not strong enough to suppress the factories." The OEM project manager also spoke up.

Then, other team members also expressed the reason why they discussed the problem privately instead of in an open meeting. There was no formal meeting system in the company, and everyone communicated by private phone calls or one-on-one, with no team coordination. I asked them to write down the problems and put them on the flipchart.

As the discussion progressed on topics where opinions were more divergent or dispersed, everyone was invited to share, including participants who had previously expressed fewer opinions. The power of this direct dialogue was immense. At first the GM was the loudest, but slowly, as more and more opinions that differed from his were expressed, he stopped rebutting others with a strong voice and began to listen and take notes.

When analyzing the Pulsometer question: **The problem can be discussed, yes - but we don't solve them. Nothing happened.** The dialogue once again showed the contradictory state of their daily work. Three participants chose to disagree, two chose not to know and two chose to agree. This time I started with the two who didn't know and asked them to clarify their choices. They expressed that the issue would indeed be discussed, but as to whether it would be resolved or not, they didn't know and no one had informed them, so they chose not to know. This time the GM didn't hold back again, he just tapped the table and asked, *"No one has informed you, so you can't just go and ask yourselves! Waiting day after day, money doesn＇t grow on trees!"*

"I'd ask, but I can't find you!" The administration manager muttered.

The head of R&D didn't make peace this time, but expressed her opinion directly, *"Indeed, sometimes I hear that there is a problem between sales and outsourcing, but the problem is only discussed between the two departments, as for how to solve the problem and how to avoid such a problem the next time, we really don't know either. To put it simply, everyone is so busy working that it seems like we don't even have formal meetings to discuss or communicate work progress, combining I'm not in the company every day, so I have to choose not to know."*

To avoid falling into silence again, I rushed to join the dialogue, *"Thank you both for what you have just shared. In your sharing, I heard once again that everyone is busy, too busy to communicate, too busy to sit down together and have a chat. As said at the beginning of the workshop in the morning, 'Finally, a time for all of us to sit down together '. I understand that we are all busy in our daily work with one person acting as 3, but now I hear that such busyness actually hinders the efficiency of our team. Team members who agree, how about your ideas?"*

The reason for the Sales Manager, who agreed to my statement, was simply that the problem really had not been solved, such as the previously discussed problem with the delivery date.

In addition to the previous payment issue not being resolved, the OEM Project manager, who agreed as well, also mentioned communication problems with the sales and finance departments. He said that he was a wimp, and even though he had thought of some solutions before communicating with the finance department, he quickly gave up all his preparations every time the finance department rejected his first proposal.

The finance manager showed a surprised expression when she heard him saying that, and she opened her mouth halfway before jokingly asking, *"Are you saying that because you think I'm like a tigress?"*

Everyone laughed and everyone was more relaxed than before. Based on the analysis and problems, I guided them to develop a work plan to improve the team's efficiency. There was a commitment of the GM to communicate more. That's not easy for a middle-aged male leader in China. In fact, he had already realized his problems and wanted to improve, but in public, his pride would not allow him to make a direct commitment to change. The team members were well aware of this.

My Reflection:

1. In fact, strong management style of the boss is a common characteristic of local enterprises in China, not only in start-ups, but also in many large enterprises. In Chinese culture, we embody collectivism, but for a team to achieve success, there must be a strong leader to lead. But a strong leader might squeeze the initiative and creativity of team members. So, it's critical for the leader to find a balance between leading and empowering his employees.

2. During the workshop, I was sometimes restricted by the Chinese "face" culture and could not ask more direct and effective questions. If I could have asked the GM directly whether he was aware of his strong management style and how it affected the team when the issue of "too strong management style" was repeated, I would have guided them to produce more outputs and made more changes. However, in Chinese culture, this kind of open and direct questioning is considered a taboo.

3. I always believed in and followed the Pulsometer (Situational Analysis) Facilitator Guide. The process of the tool is designed so that disagreements and differences are presented to the participants and dialogue occurs naturally. Even in local Chinese companies, where hierarchy is obvious occasionally, open dialogue can occur as the process progresses.

3.5. IKEA and Four Rooms of Change

Anna Wilson

IKEA has been using the Four Rooms of Change since late 1990, with success.

Responsible for the implementation at IKEA was Tomas Oxelman, who together with Claes and Ulla Janssen developed the Four Rooms of Change - furnished by IKEA.

The model became a sensation at IKEA, where no other model has received even close to that kind of coverage. Tomas Oxelman himself was surprised at how a model can have such an impact, despite only working with a simple scaled-down version, with the result that many people have a limited understanding. But perhaps that is what made it so popular. Tomas noticed that most people could quickly familiarize themselves with the basics and that it is a must today if so, many people are to catch on.

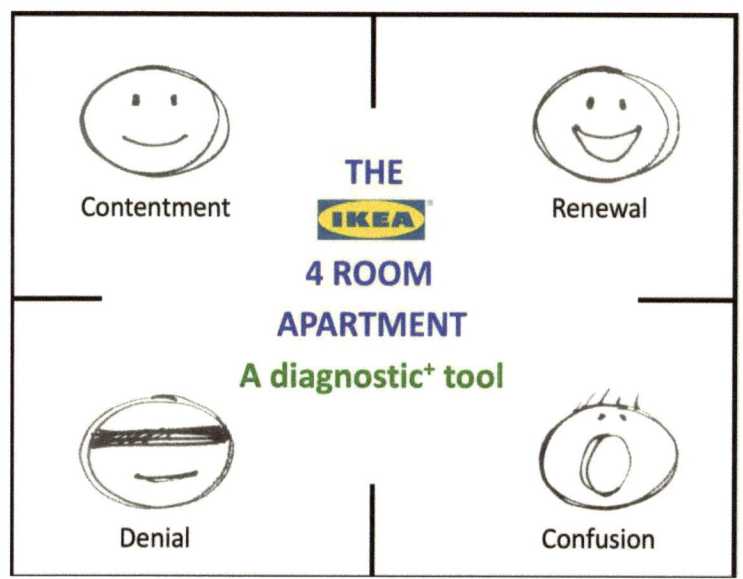

IKEA's founder Ingvar Kamprad was particularly fond of the Confusion room. He said that it is precisely in the room of confusion that we weigh different options and solutions and ask ourselves many constructive opposing questions. But only after we have reached the zero point in the room of Confusion.

Since then, the model has been used extensively worldwide, with the aim of creating an understanding of how both individuals, groups and organizations work, primarily in terms of organizational development. To be able to ask yourself as an organization the strategically important questions that are in the different rooms. This ensures that you do not miss or overlook important factors in the development and change work.

3.6. Corporate Health – Preventing psychosocial ill-health in the workplace

Anna Wilson

In the work of maintaining laws, requirements and rules regarding the employees' responsibility to prevent and work with psychosocial ill-health, it has often been shown that the work is not fully successful. Studies show that there is a lack of achieving the transformation required for these necessary changes in processes and leadership as well as in employees. With the help of Janssen's Model, the Four Rooms of Change and its tools have contributed to successful transformations.

The knowledge of what happens to us individuals, groups and organizations has contributed to increased understanding, security, stability and communication. The model helps to lead and communicate more successfully both before and during a change process. It is easier to uncensor any unwanted situations that arise, but also to ask the critical questions needed to prevent or more easily handle these situations.

It also increases the opportunity to dive deeper into the analysis from the results of the employee surveys and identify critical parts in the various business areas.

Our natural defense mechanisms that want to protect us from discomfort and criticism, sometimes knock out our rational, creative and solution-focused ability. By acquiring good change knowledge, both leaders, managers and employees have an increased chance of managing our natural defense mechanisms. This will result in a much more open climate and easier communication between management, managers, employees and departments. This is the result we most often see when we implement this change knowledge in organizations.

A more summary result is that we see The Four Rooms of Change enable the transformation that is necessary for successful change projects and by working with the model prevent psychosocial ill-health in the workplace.

3.7. Function as a Management team without a CEO in car dealer organization

Anna Wilson

This example is about showing how the model has transformed a dysfunctional management team.

The company had a couple of tough years with high dissatisfaction around management and the CEO. There was a lot of talk in the corridors and silent meetings, and in the boardroom, there was only talk about the dissatisfied employees and the lack of good leadership from managers and leaders.

The current CEO resigned, leaving a management team that had no experience whatsoever of either leading or taking joint decisions as a management team. They were at a loss.

When the management team was given the Four rooms of change as a model to work from, they began to open. Insights, understanding, and as a help in communication, the group started to function as a management team, without a CEO.

Individuals developed and so did the group. The model was used in every meeting and eventually led to creative successful operational and strategic meetings.

When a new CEO was recruited to the company, he became part of a well-functioning management team and was initiated into the model.

I asked them what the difference was from before they used the model.

They answered that it was much easier to look at their situation objectively. It was also no problem to identify their weaknesses and strengths. Questioning their own work processes became natural and acceptance was easier than before. From that it became motivating to set new goals and challenge themselves. Communication, they thought had improved but at the beginning they could not really explain why Now they know that the model is a powerful tool to use when it comes to knowing what, how and when to communicate.

The current CEO found another workplace and flourished as a manager in a different organization. Win-win.

3.8. The Four Rooms of Change in school

Anna Wilson

In 2002, Claes Janssen's wife, Ulla Janssen, conducted a study at Uppsala University[1] about her work with The Four Rooms of Change in School. The aim of the research was to investigate whether it is possible to use the Four Rooms of Change to build a common language for emotions with the children and to highlight and practice more competences in them. Mainly on the children's ability to feel empathy, as well as create security in the children's groups.

Ulla Janssen adapted the content of the model and the implementation for children that became useful for all ages of school age.

The results of the study showed that it was clearly possible to transfer the theoretical method and build the model with children. They also got a clear result that showed that the children became engaged and enthusiastic. In the interviews, the children talked about the importance of knowing how their classmates are feeling to understand why they do what they do, and to be serious in your way towards a classmate who is not feeling so well.

We know that any way of working that gives children the opportunity to actively practice understanding and expressing their emotions is good for the children. Learning does not take place separately from the children's feelings. Being emotionally competent is just as important for learning as teaching other basic subjects, such as numeracy and reading.

Other effects and observations made by Ulla Janssen were that the children's work capacity increased, the learning ability improved, and increased job satisfaction in the classes.

Based on the evaluations, the results were clearly positive in terms of the children's emotional and social competence, their behaviour in and out of the classroom and their learning ability in general.

As a teacher, it also emerged that the teacher experienced their own individual positive development, which among other things improved their way of seeing more competences in their students. They themselves felt more professional and open in their professional role.

I myself, who have a previous professional career as a principal and head of school, carried out visits and interviews to the schools that worked with the four rooms of change in their classes. The discoveries I made there amazed me and wished I had known the theory and model during the years I was working in school.

My Reflections: The benefit of the Four Rooms of Change in school was greater than I imagined.

I discovered a number of different levels and areas of activity with the model in school. This provides a development of the entire school's activities. The activities of the work teams are developed, and the management of stress increases the ability to balance stability and change in a healthy way. Increasing responsibility and thus increased job satisfaction among both children and adults in school. They work continuously and actively to eliminate the basis for offensive treatment and discrimination, a sharp reduction in bullying.

By constantly keeping track of the current situation and through a joint mapping, it leads to a common ground that contributes effectively to the creation of e.g. equality plans and other governing documents and their implementation. Through newfound self-awareness, trust increases and thus the willingness to focus on the task at hand. This improves productivity and enables you to think more freely about the result and the way to get there.

It clarifies responsibilities and division of labour between different professional groups in the school, pupils and parents. It also clarifies the division of responsibilities between adults, students and the school management.

In summary, the experiences from the work in the classrooms, were better learning results, better classroom climate and that bullying stops completely or almost completely. The contact between teachers and individual students has generally improved significantly and the teacher sees more clearly the different needs of the students. The students show greater empathic ability in relation to others and find it easier to understand and express their own feelings and needs. The work with The Four Rooms of Change turns out that instead of believing that it takes time away from teaching, instead it gives more time.

The experience from working with adults in school is that there is more focus on the common mission and instead talking about problems in school spends more time talking about maintaining a good working climate. They have a simple tool that allows teachers and other groups to effectively work in teams. In general, much easier to handle things that were previously difficult. It also makes it easier for colleagues to give each other feedback. The school management states that they can work more systematically.

A memorable comment from some students I interviewed was that *"- You can't be stupid to someone who is in denial, that person probably doesn't feel good or is sad..."*

Another student told me that she had taken the model home and put it up on the family's fridge and then said that *"- It became much easier to get mom and dad to understand what I feel and feel..."*

Like the experiences from IKEA's organization, successful results are also achieved in schools, where the strength lies in the simplicity of the model.

Four Rooms of Change Theory and other change and development approaches

4. The Four Rooms of Change theory and other change and development approaches

This chapter describes how Four Rooms can be used to complement other established and helpful approaches to development and change. We do not see it as an either/or proposition but have found in practice that Four Rooms can make other approaches even more effective. We also want to share some fundamental thoughts to deepen the understanding of the Four Rooms Theory.

4.1 House of Change: The insufficient copy for today's challenges

Dr. Angelika Schrand

The original approach is used in many countries to support change, innovation and development processes in individuals, teams and organisations - and has often been simplified in the past.

How and why did this happen?

House of Change - not Claes Janssen's original approach

If you search the Internet, you will find many different versions of the House of Change. The four rooms are integrated into one house, which seems understandable, as Claes Janssen wrote: "Four rooms are in all of us.

Then it gets lively. The room of Contentment is not translated into contentment but is even misunderstood as "self-satisfaction". The room of Censorship/Denial is described as rejection and resistance. In the sroom of Confusion, the most crucial point in the room, the zero point, is not mentioned at all. A basement is added or a sunny balcony.

Anything is possible, but it has nothing to do with the results of Claes Janssen's research.

The question now is: how did this development come about and why is the original Four Rooms not better known? Is the House of Change really a copy, a plagiarism, and what are the main differences to the original?

Differences between the House of Change and the original

The Four Rooms were developed based on Claes Janssen's research into the two different perspectives of life.

He calls it the inner Yes/No conflict and the resulting influences on the phases of change. The Four rooms of Change were developed on this basis. The House of Change and the additional rooms are not related to Claes Janssen's scientific findings and are not necessary in practice.

In addition, they are often used incorrectly in practice. For example, managers are told that they should take their employees out of the room of contentment to achieve change. But: the room of contentment creates productivity and efficiency, and trying to put all employees in denial and despair is absurd and counterproductive.

As all change practitioners know, it is difficult to help people see that things have changed. The desire to return to "the old contentment of how things used to be" does not work. Precisely because things have changed.

It is not contentment itself that is the great challenge, but the transition from **false contentment** to a **new contentment**.

False contentment is the unconscious refusal to recognize and accept that change is necessary, and that you must then go through the room of confusion - with all the uncertainties and negative feelings. This is the only way to return to a "new contentment.

It is important that individuals go through the rooms, not organizations or teams.

For example, when an organization changes, some people are inspired because they think the new direction is right. Others think the change is right, but don't know what it means for them - and are more likely to be confused. So, everyone goes through the rooms individually.

House of Change: easy but inadequate

A key finding of Claes Janssen's research was that people deal with change differently, depending on how they view life. It is therefore wrong to assume that all people in the same situations are in the same rooms. This is especially confirmed by resilience research.

The simplistic assumption, developed in the House of Change from a management perspective, that everyone should be "taken" through the rooms at the same time is therefore not effective in managing change processes successfully.

Organizations do not move through change at the same pace. The goal is to keep as many people as possible in the rooms of Contentment and inspiration. When there is clarity about goals, strategies, and one's own role, when people can rely on each other, when there is psychological security and trust in the team, it is much easier to embrace new ideas and challenges with energy and together.

This happens in the room of inspiration. The two rooms of contentment and inspiration influence each other positively, just as the two rooms of Censorship and Confusion influence each other negatively.

A brief review of the original Janssen's Model®

Depending on the situation, we are in a different room. Our perspective on life, i.e. how much stability, security and a sense of belonging we need, or how much we want to "do the right thing", or our urge for freedom, influences HOW we walk through the rooms and how easy or difficult it is for us to make the necessary decisions. Claes Janssen calls this step the "ZERO point": the moment of letting go of the past. It is a crucial step in the change process, but one that does not occur at all in the House of Change.

Four Rooms offers a systemic approach to change that considers both the individual and the organizational level and provides tools for dealing with and managing change holistically. It is more in line with the "Leading Change" approach that has been developed over the last few decades, which goes beyond change management.

Change management is the controlled, well-planned management of a defined change process in which disruptions are avoided as much as possible, and everything is kept under control. Small, trained teams manage the project.

The House of Change as an expression of its time in change management

The House of Change was developed in the 1990s by Paul Kirkbride in collaboration with the Ashridge School. The Four Rooms of Change were simplified - and provided with additional annexes to represent the most extreme manifestations of human behaviour in change processes and to meet the requirements of change management:

To manage change projects in a planned and controlled manner, with as little disruption as possible.

In the context of change management descriptions, this simplification is understandable under the assumption that "people" can be managed in the same way as processes.

The House of Change or Change House model is a clear and helpful model for this.

Responding to the understandable desire of many to have a "how to" manual, it provides a sense of security with its very helpful recommendations on how to manage change projects so that they run as smoothly and successfully as possible.

Over the years, it has been integrated and trained in management training courses by the well-known Ashridge Business School and many other providers, was in line with the management theory of the time and had a much wider reach than the Swedish consulting company that worked with the original.

But as we all know, the reality is different, even for manageable change projects. The high failure rate of up to 70% for change projects has a lot to do with how stakeholders in different roles are involved. However, when it comes to changes that are more complex and involve many people, traditional change management methods are no longer sufficient.

Four rooms for change leaders in times of multiple crises and transformation

Change leadership focuses on the vision, strategy, and motivation associated with the implementation of a change initiative. Change leaders serve as the -engine- for these initiatives, guiding and motivating their teams throughout the implementation process. Anyone who wants to go beyond "managing" change projects and believes in the importance of involving people in change processes should use the original.

The willingness to change is strengthened right from the start. The Four Rooms of Change are not simply taught but are developed directly through one's own experience. In a process developed by Claes Janssen over a period of 7 years, the people involved worked out the Four Rooms themselves, developed a better understanding of why they act differently and have a common language to deal with the emotional level in change processes and thus allow and constructively deal with disruptions.

It is an approach that involves those affected by complex change and makes them participants, as required in classical organizational development. The approach provides change leaders and consultants with a set of tools to support individual and organizational development and the ability to change.

The House of Change is still visible everywhere on the Internet and, as Claes Janssen wrote: *"Thoughts are free".*

It is often said that the model goes back to him - but the question is: why not use the much better and more effective original?

Ashridge Business School decided in 2004 not to use the House of Change anymore. They use the original, the Four Rooms of Change!

4.2 Situational Leadership

Anna Wilson

A leader who uses the Situational leadership model, a leader who can quickly adapt his or her leadership style and approach to different employee situations and how they change. The basic model was developed in the 1960s by Paul Hersey and Ken Blanchard. It is one of the most widely used in the world, and in a few words, as a leader, you adapt your approach and working methods to the situation of an employee.

Adapting leadership to the individual needs of your employees means first assessing the situation and the employee and then switching to the style that suits them. From this perspective, the ultimate leader is the one who has the flexibility to switch between how much support or direction is needed at any given time.

To clarify what is meant by situation, it is about what internal and external factors affect the employee in a specific situation. For example, a person who is new to the job needs a different type of leadership than an experienced person who knows the organization inside out. This means that as a leader, you need to be flexible and able to change your leadership style depending on the situation.

Hersey and Blanchard argue that by letting the situation guide your leadership, you meet and support the employee at their level. Each employee has different needs, such as experience, strengths, independence, and self-confidence. Instead of applying the same leadership behaviours to everyone on the team, you adapt to best develop each person where they are in the moment.

The Situational Leadership Model

The model itself is based on four fields that represent different leadership styles and situations. But before we go through the different areas, it may be useful to have a basic understanding of how the model is supposed to work.

The focus is on the individual employee, or what Hersey and Blanchard call the follower. Therefore, the model cannot be applied to an entire organization or group of people but requires that each individual in the group reated separately. There are, of course, exceptions where one leadership style may fit several, such as a group of new employees.

As a leader, you need to be prepared to switch between different leadership styles as the situation demands, which requires a degree of flexibility.

With the model to support you, you can follow each employee's journey and evolve your leadership as the situation changes. It's like watching someone go from new hire to old hand, or from wallpaper flower to glow in the dark.

The Synergies of Both Models

To find the synergies between the situational model and the four rooms of change, let's look directly at the differences between the theories.

For example:

I am a new employee in my job role or task, my manager is guiding me based on the given work situation I am currently in.

Now, if we do not have the knowledge or know how I really feel or am according to the four rooms of change, regardless of the work situation I am in, my manager's attempts to give me the right leadership may be of no use.

Many leaders and managers trained in both models can see these synergies immediately. The key words that describe behaviours in the different rooms and phases of the models are largely identical when it comes to management/leadership.

One example was when one of the managers I coached was having difficulties with a coworker. Although the manager had good situational leadership skills, he was not able to get the employee to achieve the desired results. After the manager underwent training in the Four Rooms of Change, things started to improve. He replied that he now understood what difficulties belonged to the employee's job, as well as what difficulties belonged to the employee in general and in private and vice versa when it came to what the desired situation was for the employee.

The manager found it much easier to coach and support his employee and when he then applied the knowledge to other employees and teams, there were big differences and improved results.

Managers and leaders describe that no matter what other leadership model they use or are trained in, training in Janssen's model and the four rooms of change is invaluable.

The reason is that with the four rooms of change, you can identify where individuals, groups or organizations are in a current situation. And based on that you can apply the right leadership model for that situation. All leaders who use the model also experience that employee´s feeling of participation increases, the feeling of being both seen and listened by their manager and an increased motivation.

And they agree that everyone should receive the Four Rooms of Change as basic training and knowledge when it comes to our interpersonal relationships, communication, leadership and especially when it comes to change.

The results reported are improved understanding, better communication, faster and more efficient processes, but most importantly an increase in people's wellbeing.

4.2 Kotter´s 8-Step Change Model

Dr. Angelika Schrand, Anna Wilson

Kotter's eight-step Change Model was introduced with the aim of supporting organizations in their change work. The model was developed based on John P. Kotter's many years of experience in practical change work, in both failed and successful projects. It highlights typical problems that occur in a change process and can have devastating consequences.

These include failure to implement change, change that takes too long and costs too much, and acquisitions or mergers that fail to deliver the expected synergies.

Harvard professor Dr. John P. Kotter is one of the world's leading experts on organizational change. He wrote Leading Change in 1996 and its sequel, The Heart of Change, a few years later. He describes the eight steps to achieving desired change and the importance of involving people in the change process. Change is driven by emotional commitment rather than logical analysis and calculation, and the importance of embedding change in leadership. The 8 Steps are in a short overview:

Create a Sense of Urgency: Inspire people to act with passion and purpose to achieve a bold, aspirational opportunity.

Build a Guiding Coalition: Form a group with enough power to lead the change effort and encourage the group to work as a team.

Form a Strategic Vision and Initiatives: Create a vision to help direct the change effort and develop strategies for achieving that vision.

Enlist a Volunteer Army: Communicate the vision and strategy to as many people as possible to gain their commitment.

Enable Action by Removing Barriers: Remove obstacles to change, change systems or structures that undermine the vision.

Generate Short-Term Wins: Plan for and create short-term wins to provide evidence that the effort is paying off.

Sustain Acceleration: Use increased credibility to change systems, structures, and policies that don't fit the vision.

Institute Change: Anchor new approaches in the culture to ensure they stick.

Each step of the model describes what needs to be done to keep moving in the right direction, but also the common mistakes made in many change processes. The common thread throughout the eight steps is the importance of creating a sense of urgency throughout the process. A sense of urgency keeps the momentum going. The eight steps guide the organization through three major phases of a change process.

Even this clear roadmap, the focus on people and creating momentums by short-term wins is extremely helpful in change processes, the main critical aspect is that the model is too linear and a sequential and does not reflect the complex and iterative nature of real-world change processes. Kotter evolves his own framework into the Accelerate (XLR8) Model. In his book Accelerate he integrates a more agile, network-like structure, which allows a greater flexibility and faster response.

Completing and Fixing the Change or Completing and becoming more powerful

This model is a good practical model to use in a change process. However, what ensures the success of the transformation is the knowledge of how we as individuals, groups and organizations function in change and development. This knowledge is gained from the four rooms of change.

In every phase of a change process and in every informal or formal group we are individuals with emotions, and we are in different rooms. For people who drive change the Knowledge of the Four Rooms is extremely helpful, to make the emotional status transparent and to avoid a lot of misunderstandings and conflicts – or to deal with the conflicts in a constructive and respectful way. As you can see that the Four Rooms enables people to do their job at each step of the Change process. It supports to communicate in better way by assuming – or better by asking in which rooms they are regarding the vision, strategy, goals, decisions or the implementation plan. And it avoids putting people in a resistance box. It promotes the willingness to contribute and the ability to change in general, which is needed in times of continuous, permanent change.

Kotter's model describes what needs to be done at each stage to create participation and commitment. Experience and analysis show that we still do not really succeed with change projects, the most common figure is 25%.

We have met many managers and leaders who, despite a good model such as Kotter's 8 steps, fail to get everyone on board with the change journey. It takes more time than planned and becomes costly for both the process and the people involved.

What we see is that with the knowledge of how individuals work in change, we can also understand, respond, communicate and lead based on that knowledge. And that is why we think that Four Rooms makes the 8 Steps, or the newer 8 Accelerators, even more powerful and also provides a basis for making the organisation more capable of change and more powerful after completion of the specific change project.

4.3 Application in Coaching combined with the Solution Focus Approach

Giuliano Tarditi

In this chapter I will tell you about my experience of how I apply the Four Rooms of Change model in individual coaching.

When I took the Four Rooms certification course in 2016 I had already been a professional coach for several years and I immediately saw how the Four Rooms model represented very precisely what happens in a coaching process with a coachee.

Very often my client, my coachee, begins the coaching process to solve a problem or overcome a difficulty and is typically a bit stuck in the situation and confused about how to get out of it.

When I began to become familiar with the Four Rooms model, I saw clearly that most of my coachees as a starting point positioned themselves in the Self-Censorship room or in the Confusion.

I then began to apply my coaching practice in the context of The Four Rooms with the intention to get a client out of Self-Censorship and Confusion.

"When a coachee is in Confusion he needs to make clarity ".
One of the tools I found most useful to make clarity is the

Solution Focused Approach[1]
This technique allows the person to focus on solution instead of problem.
For example, after the coachee explains and describes her problem, you immediately ask her "What would you like instead?",
„What should happen, if things went the way you want?"
This approach makes people describe the ideal situation, the preferred future instead of focusing on problems.

A Coaching conversation according to the Solution Focused Approach

Situation
What is the problem situation?

Define Objective starting from expected results
How can I help you?
What is your objective?

*If the problem was solved, **What** would be different, just for you?*

*If the problem was solved, **How** would it be different, just for you?*

The Future preferred (or desired)

Suppose you ... were able to achieve your goals; what would you do differently in this scenario?

Suppose your boss behaved the way you wanted him to; how would you change things?

What would you do then that you are not doing now?

Signs of the Solutions (Scaling question)
IMMINENT PROGRESS

Thinking about the problem you came with today,
On a scale of 1 to 10,
10 = you have fully realized your goals, where you are now?
What makes this value to be different from 1?

Signs of progress
Imagine you were able to move to X + 1.
What will you say if you've taken a step forward on this scale?
What would you do then, you're not doing now?

Conclusion
Defining first step or action plan.

Application case in Business Coaching:

I will give you an example in business coaching. The case is real, the name is fictitious.

I meet my coachee Stefania, a manager responsible for a group of about 20 people, and she tells me about her problematic situation.

Stefania tells me that there will be a reorganization and that her department will be reduced by 3 units. In the first 20-30 minutes of our conversation Stefania tells me, or better to say, complains about the fact that her department had already undergone a reorganization 2 years ago (and also the entire company); she complains about the fact that she already has so many activities now and that she doesn't know how she will be able to carry them out with 3 fewer people. She is already under pressure, she works very long hours, she can't find the time to dedicate to her team to manage it as she would like. She says she has no time to think about strategies but is very focused on doing, doing, doing.

She says that during the previous reorganization she almost had a nervous breakdown due to the pressure on performance she had to endure. And she says she doesn't want to go through the same experience again. I ask some probing questions and she answers that "she already knows how it will end" and that "it will end like the other time".

I ask her if she has spoken about this with the boss, and she replies "No, it's useless anyway...".

She is heartbroken, almost resigned, she sees no alternative to what has already happened in the past. She has almost always spoken, and always imagining that her immediate future will be just as bad as what happened in the past.

I wanted her to set **a goal**, so I asked her. *"What would you like instead?"*

Answer: To do *the activities that can be done with fewer people, instead of doing everything we do today, with more people.*

I asked her to describe the ideal situation, the preferred future: *"Can you describe to me what happens, if things go the way you want?"* (remember: talk in present tense, as it is happening now)

Answer: *We agree with the boss and the board on the priority projects and we'll do them. As we receive more requests for projects, especially from the Board, we agree on what to move forward with among the activities we are doing today and we reorganize the priorities.*

I asked her to establish a first action: *"What is the first thing to do to go in the direction you just described?"*

Answer: *"I have to agree on the priorities with the boss: determine which are the most important projects and start doing them first. And second, we go to a meeting to align the priorities with with the Board, before starting to work on the projects.*

I ask about differences: **"What is different for you in this scenario?**

Answer: *"I have to agree on priorities with my boss instead of just starting to execute whatever task I receive!"*

In this conversation we focus on "what you want", not on the problem. I as a coach skipped away from going deeper into the problem. Most of the time is invested in making the coachee to have a clear vision of the preferred future. A typical sequence of questions goes as:

"Describe me how you imagine the new situation… and tell me more,…and what else, …what people around you do…and what you do …"

The energy in coaching is different because we do not focus on the problem but on what the coachee wants. It is important to be as specific as possible with the *vision of the preferred future* to link the associated positive emotions. The Four Rooms enable the coachee to locate themselves and the solution-oriented focus makes it possible to walk through the doors between the rooms.

4.4 Sustainability. Four Rooms meets Inner Development Goals (IDGs)

Birgit Freitag

Sustainability is inextricably linked to change - not arbitrary change, but complex, far-reaching and systemic change, the effects of which often only become apparent in the medium to distant future - in other words, transformation.

Embedding sustainability in the long term therefore requires change that applies the principles of transformation to the context of sustainability.

The methodological approaches of classical change have their place in transformation, but they are not sufficient. This profound change requires more than methodological approaches; it requires a fundamental change of attitude.

At the same time, the importance of sustainability for organizations is becoming increasingly important (for survival), making the transformation into a sustainable organization inevitable for a secure, regenerative future.

Yet despite the need and urgency, we are often slow to act. This is where the Four Rooms of Change, in combination with the

Inner Development Goals (IDGI), provide a valuable framework for making this change concrete and achievable.

Why do we find it so difficult to act sustainably?

Sustainability and sustainable transformation, as a cross-cutting issue, taps into all the aspects that trigger our mental defenses: it is complex, it requires a change of mindset to achieve the desired results, and these results will only have an impact in the long term, but they require current, short-term, comprehensive decisions and actions.

We experience reactions such as fear of loss and uncertainty, feel an apparent mismatch between what is required of us and what we are willing to give, based on an attitude that sees change as a threat rather than an opportunity ('What is change worth for?').

Our neurobiological and psychological survival mechanisms (defenses), which have evolved over millions of years, can become obstacles in the context of sustainable change. They literally stand in the way of the action needed for a regenerative future.

As a result, we find it difficult to take action to actively shape changes. This is where inner development comes in: Being aware of our defenses is the starting point for change and new behaviors.

Inner development encompasses our thought patterns, values and attitudes, which are expressed in our emotional experience and behavior. But where does this development lead? What indsets, attitudes, values and skills are needed to make the desired changes possible?

Orientation and compass by linking the Inner development Goals and Four Rooms of Change

The **Inner Development Goals (IDGs)** provide valuable guidance for inner development. The IDGs are an initiative (NGO) dedicated to the dissemination and promotion of science-based skills and qualities that support us on an individual and collective level to lead meaningful, sustainable and productive lives, thus contributing to the achievement of the Sustainable Development Goals (SDGs). The 17 SDGs - Sustainable Development Goals - provide the external target framework. Achieving these goals requires internal development, which is provided by 23 key competencies and qualities (the IDGs): 'internal development for external change'.

These are grouped into five clusters: being, thinking, relating, collaborating and acting

The IDG Framework [1] presents the skills and qualities of the 5 clusters

| 1 Being | 2 Thinking | 3 Relating | 4 Collaborating | 5 Acting |
Relationship to Self	Cognitive Skills	Caring for Others and the World	Social Skills	Enabling Change
Inner Compass	Critical Thinking	Appreciation	Communication Skills	Courage
Integrity and Authenticity	Complexity Awareness	Connectedness	Co-creation Skills	Creativity
Openness and Learning Mindset	Perspective Skills	Humility	Inclusive Mindset and Intercultural Competence	Optimism
Self-awareness	Sense-making	Empathy and Compassion	Trust	Perseverance
Presence	Long-term Orientation and Visioning		Mobilisation Skills	

This inner development is an essential element of controlled, active transformation, rather than letting it happen passively - in the spirit of A. Novy „Change by Design instead of Disaster." [2]

But what does inner development mean and how do we access these inner qualities?

Claes Janssen's Four Rooms of Change model offers a valuable approach to understanding and classifying the emotional and cognitive responses (behavior) to change. A compass that provides information about our inner state.

This model makes it clear that we are constantly in one of Four Rooms -contentment, censorship, confusion or inspiration. Each of these has an essential function in the change process.

As an -emotional pulse check-, the model helps us to stop and ask ourselves:
How do I feel right now?
Where do I stand?
How do I perceive the change?
What new space will open if I am willing to change my perspective and 'open the doors' between the rooms?

The model also illustrates how two fundamental attitudes to life - as poles of a dialectical scale (personal dialectics) - influence our reactions and movement between the rooms. Awareness of this dynamic promotes understanding of different perspectives along the scale and their impact, thus creating the basis for constructive dialogue and consensus.

The combination of inner development and change competence - supported by the IDGs and the Four Rooms of Change - opens up a clearer way of understanding sustainable transformation in a structured way, not as an external fiat, but as a personal and collective design task. The Transformation Matrix was created from this.

Application to individual and collective transformation

The Transformation Matrix reflects the observed correlation between the fundamental attitudes of life and the dynamics of change, represented as levels of maturity (stages of development) of individual and organizational consciousness.

Basic Framework Transformation Matrix (with 5 levels of maturity, see description below)

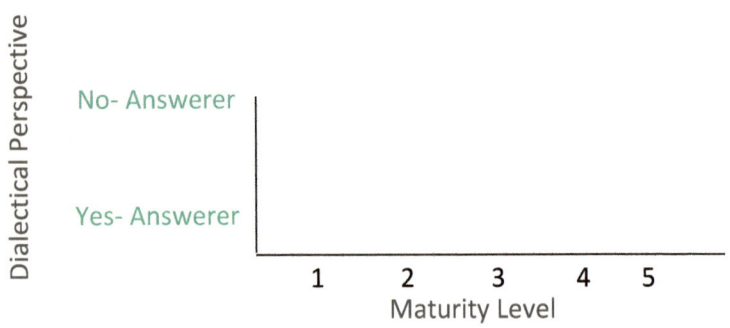

Horizontal: Maturity Scale: Stages of Consciousness Development
The scale is divided into three clusters with five levels of maturity:

Cluster 1 - Awareness: (Maturity Level 1+2)

Room of Censorship

1. Unconscious Censorship:
Unconscious-unreflective: Changes are ignored or actively denied; existing patterns remain untouched.
2. Conscious Censorship
Conscious passive: Initial awareness of the need for change, but no active action.

Cluster 2 - First practical actions: (Maturity Level 3+4)

Room of Confusion

3. Confusion
Searching and learning: Active exploration of new concepts, accompanied by uncertainty and experimentation.

Room of inspiration

4. Inspiration
Conscious and committed: Increasing inner clarity and responsibility go hand in hand with concrete, inspiring action.

Cluster 3 - Sustainability as lived practice: (Maturity Level 5)

Room of Contentment

5. Anchoring and shaping: Proactive, resilient and open attitude towards change.

Mapping the Four Rooms to the Transformation Matrix maturity levels shows overlap:

The Four Rooms of Change can therefore be used as a maturity scale and as a quick guide:

As an x-axis, they map the long-term development of an individual or an organization and make it possible to visualize progress in dealing with change and sustainability (sustainable transformation). Within a phase, the 'Four Rooms of Change' serve as a 'pulse check' of the current situation.

In both cases, targeted development measures can be derived: The room and maturity level position influence which IDG competencies can or should be activated to enable the next step on the maturity scale.

Vertical: The influence of personal dialectics on sustainable action

Claes Janssen's personal dialectics describe the attitude to life and therefore to change, which significantly influences the development dynamics (reactions and speed) along the maturity scale.

- **NO- Answerer:** Orientation towards stability, security and belonging.
- **YES- Answerer:** Openness to personal responsibility, searching for freedom and innovation.

Neither attitude is better or worse; both are essential. Mental flexibility - the ability to consciously adopt different positions depending on the context - is a sign of increasing maturity. Increasing maturity, in turn, is a prerequisite for constructive dialogue as a precondition for the all-important consensus.

The combined powerful approach: Four Rooms and IDG Competencies in the Transformation Matrix

Dialectical Scale	IDG Competencies				
YES- Anwerer	Empathy Perspective Skills (acceptance of "Yes")	Creativity Critical Thinking	Creativity Collaboration	Perspective Skills Resilience	Creativity Collaboration
Balanced distributed answers (transition)	Self awareness Resilience (first uncertainties)	Resilience Collaboration	Resilience Critical Thinking	Collaboration Creativity	Perspective Skills Empathy
NO -Answerer	Self awareness Compassion (for security)	Empathy Critical Thinking (edit doubts)	Perspective Skills (evaluate stability) Self awareness (about think-pattern)	Critical Thinking Empathy (affiliation)	Self awareness Collaboration
Four Rooms Transformation Level of Maturity	Censorship Unconsciously-unreflected	Censorship Conscious-passive	Confusion Searching and learning	Inspiration Conscious and committed	Contentment Anchored and creative
	1	2	3	4	5

Understanding and using diversity of perspectives

As awareness grows, the ability to integrate different perspectives increases:

- Maturity Level 1-2: Fixation on one's own position; change of perspective is perceived as a threat.
- Maturity level 3-4: Growing openness and realization that diversity of perspective broadens the horizon.
- Maturity Level 5: Diversity of perspective is used as a resource to develop innovative and sustainable solutions.

The resulting matrix combines the maturity scale (horizontal) and the personal dialectic (vertical). The resulting development areas provide a basis for the targeted allocation of IDG competencies.

The Four Rooms Transformation matrix and IDG- Allocation:

1. Predominantly NO-Answerer
   - Focus: Stability, security and trust.
   - IDGs: promoting awareness of one's own patterns and empathy.
2. Balanced yes/no distributed answerers - middle position.
   - Focus: Dealing with uncertainty and tension.
   - IDGs: resilience, critical thinking and collaboration.
3. Predominantly YES-Answerer:
   - Focus: personal responsibility, innovation and design.
   - IDGs: creativity, changing perspectives and collaboration.

What the interaction between the IDG framework and the Four Rooms of Change can look like in concrete terms is shown below using two formats: application in a professional context and then application in a personal context.

Application in a professional context: team leadership and organizational development

In organizations that are striving for a sustainable transformation by consistently aligning their business processes with sustainability, the IDGs can serve as a 'toolbox' to strengthen managers and teams in a targeted manner. This raises awareness of sustainable behavior in terms of strategic orientation.

The 'Four Rooms of Change' enable managers to identify the emotional state of their teams and promote IDG skills:

Contentment:
Although some employees feel comfortable with the current structure, they are very aware of the critical situation and would like to develop options for action.

→ Encourage creativity, perseverance and communication skills to generate ideas, persist in implementing them and win over others.

Censorship:
Others resist change - perhaps out of fear of losing their jobs or a lack of understanding of new requirements.
→ Build trust through self-awareness, empathy and appreciation.

Confusion:
Some employees recognize the need for change but feel overwhelmed by the multitude of demands.
→ Building resilience and self-efficacy to provide direction and security.

Inspiration:
Some employees are actively involved in the change process.
→ Create spaces for innovation and collaboration to encourage creative solutions.

Managers can use the Four Rooms of Change as a **'team pulse check'** and strengthen individual IDG competencies. The progress of the transformation - whether at individual, team or organizational level - can be measured against a maturity scale and developed in a targeted way.

Personal application: sustainable lifestyles

IDGs also provide a valuable framework for actively tackling change in the private sphere. Imagine a person who wants to make their lifestyle more sustainable, for example by reducing their carbon footprint. In combination with the 'Four Rooms of Change', the IDGs can work as follows:

Contentment:
The person lives very consciously, i.e. sustainability is very present for them and wants to achieve even more in line with the sustainable requirements.
→ Encouraging communication skills and perseverance to enroll others.

Censorship:
Initial impulses to change are met with resistance as they are perceived as exhausting or restrictive.
→ Developing compassion - for self and others - to overcome blocks.

Confusion:
The person recognizes the need for change but feels overwhelmed by the variety of measures.
→ Support through complex problem solving and resilience to identify feasible steps.

Inspiration:
Initial successes motivate the person to expand their commitment and take others with them.
→ Encouraging collaboration and creativity to bring sustainable lifestyles to the community.

Conclusion 1: Change as a dynamic process

The 'Four Rooms of Change' allow us to understand change not as a linear, but as a dynamic, emotional process. Every person - and every organization - moves through these rooms in their own way.

The IDGs provide a kind of a toolbox from which the appropriate skills and qualities can be selected to support inner development, depending on the individual status or maturity level of a team, organization or individual.

Transformation thus becomes a conscious, manageable journey - in both professional and personal contexts.

Conclusion 2: Transformation tools allow you to accompany and shape sustainable development

Linking the 'Four Rooms of Change' with the Inner development goals (IDG) results in a comprehensive set of tools to support and shape sustainable transformation development:

- The Transformation Matrix: Assessing the current situation and managing inner development in an individual and organizational context.
- The 'Four Rooms of Change' model: change formula, emotional pulse check, mirror of consciousness maturity levels and impulse generator for the next development steps.
- IDG: competencies and qualities that support inner development.

Conscious inner development makes it easier to deal with mental defences and enables us to take active action for a sustainable future.

4.5 The Change Curve and the Four Rooms-Contradiction or Complement?

Wiebke Steinel

The theory of the Four Rooms of Change and the process of its introduction has already shown the importance of dealing with emotions in change processes.

In Change Management, a well-known and often applied model is the Change Curve developed by Elisabeth Kübler-Ross. The Swiss American psychiatrist studied the emotional and social experience of dying or the death of a loved one (Kübler-Ross (1969): On Death and Dying). The transition theorist Sugarman later investigated emotional responses in various contexts. The phase descriptions that follow are based on this research and are widely used in organizational development.

As already described in Chapter 1, Claes Janssen referred to several other theories to develop the movement through the Four Rooms, namely scientists such as Cullberg, Levinson and Rossi. Although Claes Janssen did not refer to the scientific results of Elisabeth Kübler-Ross, both models fit together and support each other.

The Change Curve is a model with seven phases:

The first phase is shock as a reaction to the announcement of change. It can be equated with suddenly leaving the Room of Contentment.

The next phase is denial. Here you believe that the change is not relevant to you or your work environment. This is the unconscious part of the Room of Censorship where you do not want to acknowledge that you are affected.

The third stage is called awareness, as you realize that the change affects you, which leads you to block or resist the change. You may become angry, upset, or blame others.

This is the conscious part of the Room of Censorship, and these are typical behaviors seen in teams.

The next phase is acceptance, the time when reality is acknowledged, and you begin to let go of comfortable past habits. Confidence and productivity are low in this phase, and it represents the low point of the Change Curve. This point is also known as the valley of tears that you must cross.

The theory of the Four Rooms of Change looks at this phase in a more nuanced way. Initially, the transition from the Room of Censorship to the Room of Confusion is the first impulse to change something about the situation. And the subsequent wandering in the Room of Confusion and the crossing of the Zero Point, the moment to really let go of the past, show how crucial this phase is and that it consists of several steps.

The fifth phase is called exploration, where new approaches and skills are tried out, and attempts are made to do things differently. An initial engagement with change takes place and perhaps a tentative commitment emerges.

In the Room of Confusion, this phase corresponds to the part beyond the Zero Point, when new options and possibilities suddenly become visible and the upwind of change takes hold.

The sixth phase is the search for meaning, characterized by a positive view of the future. You reorganize your work and learn to deal with the changed situation.

This phase corresponds to the Room of Inspiration, in which you try out, test, and try to shape and implement the courageously chosen option in such a way that it represents a real solution that can bring you back to the Room of Contentment.

The seventh and final phase of the Change Curve is integration. Here the situation is no longer new, and you know how things are going.

This is the transition from the Room of Inspiration to the Room of Contentment, the harvesting of the fruits of the change that has taken place, the flow that Claes Janssen describes, when things interlock again and are transferred into a new routine.

The shape of the Change Curve demonstrates that upon completion of the process, self-perceived competence has increased in comparison to the starting point. There are fluctuations in between, yet it is clear that change is advantageous due to the experience gained and the new skills acquired.

Originally developed as a linear curve, Kübler-Ross published a graph with overlapping circles in 1978 to show that the different stages are not necessarily a linear experience. [1] This further development underlines Claes Janssen's approach to moving continuously through the Four Rooms. A permanent stabilization at the end is not possible and especially the increase in the number but also the speed of changes in our environment makes this clear. The intention of accelerating the speed and reducing the amplitude at which individuals and teams in organizations go through the Change Curve makes sense for supporting employees in change processes. This is also where Claes Janssen comes in. However, it is important to understand that you cannot push anyone through the rooms but can only offer support and create framework conditions that enable individuals to open doors and follow their personal path through the rooms.

Communication is considered a key success factor in change processes and is a lever for guiding employees through the Change Curve and the Four Rooms. The Change Curve and its various phases can be used to highlight which type of communication or information is relevant at which point in time. **Clarity** is particularly important in the first two phases. Communication can be largely formalized and directed at larger target groups, e.g. in the form of town hall meetings or written communication via communication channels established within the company. Transparency about the reasons for, the objectives of and the path to change are relevant contents here.

The next two phases are primarily about **emotional support**. This is based on the personal position of the employees in the change process and requires a stronger dialog in a 1:1 format, for example in the form of employee dialog. The aim is to find out what needs are driving the behavior and what measures can be taken to address them individually.

The last three phases primarily require **orientation and support**. Emphasizing the vision once again, setting guidelines for the choice of options and exemplifying and establishing a culture of failure are crucial here. It is about exploring, trying things out and experimenting. Mistakes are made in the process, which shape the right personal path and are part of learning and development. Whether for the organization or the individual, it is about finding out what works and can be established and consolidated as a new standard in the future to be productive again and achieve wellbeing.

The two models complement each other, although in my opinion the Change Curve is too simplistic in some points. The realization that everyone goes through the Four Rooms or the Change Curve at a different pace illustrates the challenge of accompanying an entire organization through change. Janssen's Model® offers the Pulsometer, an instrument to measure the intensity of the Four Rooms of Change and to conduct a qualitative dialog based on the quantitative results. In this way, suitable measures to increase wellbeing and productivity can be defined and implemented. This measurability and form of support offers a great advantage for organizational development.

5. Conclusion and you want to know: How to use it?

We hope you enjoyed the journey through the different steps. Four Rooms of Change - the formula for change! When we were thinking about the title, we were reluctant to use the phrase The Change Formula. Let's not use another Bullshit Bingo expression was our first thought. After thinking about it and summarising all the applications and different areas we use it in - we said to ourselves - yes - it works for everyone - people of different ages and it doesn't matter what degree they have. We use it in China, Europe, Africa, America and Australia - everywhere... with teams and different kinds of social systems. So - we are convinced - it is the right expression. The theory is easy to understand and the process of creating the Four Rooms with people works! It is amazing and even after years of working with it - it is still great to see how it works.

In times of constant crisis and polarisation within society, it's even more important to be able to develop and change. We can only face these challenges if we work together, if we are able to treat and communicate with each other in a way that respects our different "views on life".

Would you like to experience it and learn how to work with it?

6. Bibliography and Remarks

The following books, which are not available in bookstores were used as sources:

> The Four Rooms of Change
> Part I
> A Practical Everyday Psychology- 2nd ed.
> 2011 © Claes Janssen

The Four Rooms of Change
Part II
Fifteen More Years of Experience
2011 © Claes Janssen

For the reason of clarity, only Part I or II is mentioned below. In addition, the theory manual Personal Dialectic by Janssen's Model(R) is used, which is issued by participants as part of the certification process.

> Theory Booklet Personal Dialectics
> 2021   Janssen´s Model®

1. The Story of the Development of the Four Rooms Theory
1. Part II, P 37
2. Part 1, P 109
3. Part I, P 109
4. Theory Booklet, P19
5. Part I, P 35
6. Theory Booklet, P 19
7. Part 1, P 16
8. Part 1, P 20

9. Theory Booklet, P 7
10. Part 1, P24
11. Theory Booklet, P 10
12. Part 1, P 26. This is an extract. Detailed information will be found in Chapter 2.3
13. Part 1. P 26
14. Theory Booklet, P21
15. It is often stated in publications that the Four Rooms of Change are based on Ruth Kübler Ross theory. The development of the theory shows that this is not the case - Claes Janssen also quotes other sources for the "Movements".
16. Part 1, P27
17. Part 1, P 31
18. Part 1, P 32
19. Part 1, P 205
20. Part 1, P 208

2. The Theory: Practical Everyday Psychology

1. Theory Booklet, P 24
2. Part 1, P 26
3. Part 1, P27
4. Theory Booklet, 17
5. Part 1, P 220
6. Quote of Marvin Weisboard in Theory Booklet, P 11
7. Part 1, P220

3. Four Rooms in Practise

1. Ulla Janssen (grade schoolteacher and married to Claes) begins to work with the Four Rooms of Chane in the Classroom, with eight years olds first. In 2002 she presents her paper "Psychology in the Classroom" as an examination work in medial teaching (Part I, P343)

4. Four Rooms and other Theories

4.3.

1. Adapted by Giuliano Tarditi. Based on: Peter Szabo and Daniel Meier, Brief Coaching, Mindware Publishing; Paul Jackson and Mark McKergow, *The Solution Focus,* Nicholas Brealey International

4.4.

1. The IDG Framework you can find: <u>Framework – Inner Development Goals</u>

2. The announcement for a course by Andreas Novy reads: *
"Don't deny change, shape it: 'The only sure thing is that it won't stay the way it is"-

3. Maturity Model: Following and modified: Richard Garret: 7 levels of consciousness

5. https://www.ekrfoundation.org/5-stages-of-grief/5-stages-grief.

7. Authors and Co-Authors

Dr. Angelika Schrand

She studied political science and sociology and holds a doctorate in philosophy. Her main interest is how individuals and social systems develop and how to increase the capability to change. As a Managing Director of CONTUR she developed CONTUR as a shareholder from the very beginning. Experiences in various HR Function incl. VP/HR Role or HR Director in different companies enriched her professional background. Her passion topic is Change & Transformation. As a Certified Global Program Leader for Janssen´s Model® she is working with the Theory since 2017 and acquired the partnership with Janssen´s Model® for CONTUR.

Anna Wilson

Anna Wilson, owner of Janssen´s Model and Wilson Utveckling AB. Her areas of expertise are in leadership development, Change Management and is a certified business- and leadership coach. She has worked with the Four rooms of change since 2014 and took over the copyright to the Four rooms of change from Claes Janssen 2021. Claes Janssen and Anna decided to run the model under the new brand Janssen´s Model. Over 30 years of experience as a manager, change management, team development and coaching of both individuals and management teams.

Birgit Freitag

Her professional background includes a degree in chemical engineering specialising in nuclear and biochemistry as well as business administration and information technology.

She has been a certified coach for contextual individual and business coaching since 2011 and has continued her training in systemic organisational development and change management (ISB Wiesloch). With many years of experience in the corporate environment, particularly in project management, as well as a certified qualification in the Four Rooms of Change® Certification Program, she brings a broad range of skills to the table. She is certified as a transformation consultant at the Academy for Transformation Design in Berlin.

Wiebke Steinel

Wiebke studied the topics of organizational development, strategy and innovation management. She worked as an Internal Consultant for HR and Organizational Development at a hidden champion. As responsible for Corporate Development and Culture Manager she managed various internal Projects to develop and anchor the Culture Development and Innovation Processes. As a Head of Organizational Development & Process Management at a medium sized company she was able to advance her knowledge in strategy and Leadership as well as Agile project management, digital transformation and process optimization. Using her knowledge in a different role, she is working as a trainer and consultant at CONTUR. She is a Certified User of Janssen´s Model since 2023 and responsible within CONTUR for Janssens's Model.®.

Giuliano Tarditi

 Giuliano has over 20 years of experience as a Trainer and Executive Coach. He is specialized in methodologies for the development and transformation of professional behaviours for Executives, managers and entrepreneurs with a strongly experiential approach. As an active member of ICF Italia and he was the Project Leader for the ICF Coaching Expo 2021 and Project Leader for the ICF Coaching Conference 2022, the most important events in Italy dedicated to Coaching. He is a member of the ICF Global Executive and Leadership Coaching Community of Practice.

Jens Witte

At the beginning of his professional development, he was an executive in various positions in commercial enterprises for many years, including Head of Technology Competence Center and Senior Manager Service and Production. In his current position as a trainer and consultant at CONTUR GmbH, his work focuses on the design and implementation of management development programs, train-the-trainer measures, seminars and workshops on virtual learning, service excellence, team development measures and moderation. He is a Certified User of Four Rooms of Change- Janssen´s Model® since 2019.

Dr. Doris Yuan

Doris Yuan's professional background includes a PhD in Psychology, and she has more than 25 years of experience in various HR and operational functions in different industries. Together with other Coaches she drives the Inner Development Goals (IDG´s) Movement in China. She is a certified Leadership Coach; PCC and a certified user of Janssen's model, using the Four Rooms of Change in her coaching and team development client projects.